PENGUIN BOOKS — GREAT FOOD

Recipes from the White Hart Inn

WILLIAM VERRALL was publican of the White Hart in Lewes, Sussex, from 1737 to 1760. Having been apprenticed to the French chef St Clouet, Verrall created recipes that were an inspired combination of the French and English traditions standing apart from those of his contemporaries. Published in 1759, the ideas in his *Complete System of Cookery* are strikingly modern, and many dishes – which include turkey braised with chestnuts, rabbit with champagne and ham hock with peach fritters – would not be out of place on restaurant menus today.

Recipes from the White Hart Inn

WILLIAM VERRALL

PENGUIN BOOKS

PENGUIN BOOKS

Published by the Penguin Group
Penguin Books Ltd, 80 Strand, London WC2R 0RL, England
Penguin Group (USA) Inc., 375 Hudson Street, New York, New York 10014, USA
Penguin Group (Canada), 90 Eglinton Avenue East, Suite 700, Toronto, Ontario,
Canada M4P 2Y3 (a division of Pearson Penguin Canada Inc.)
Penguin Ireland, 25 St Stephen's Green, Dublin 2, Ireland
(a division of Penguin Books Ltd)
Penguin Group (Australia), 250 Camberwell Road,
Camberwell, Victoria 3124, Australia
(a division of Pearson Australia Group Pty Ltd)
Penguin Books India Pvt Ltd, 11 Community Centre,
Panchsheel Park, New Delhi – 110 017, India
Penguin Group (NZ), 67 Apollo Drive, Rosedale, Auckland 0632, New Zealand
(a division of Pearson New Zealand Ltd)
Penguin Books (South Africa) (Pty) Ltd, 24 Sturdee Avenue,
Rosebank, Johannesburg 2196, South Africa

Penguin Books Ltd, Registered Offices: 80 Strand, London WC2R 0RL, England

www.penguin.com

A Complete System of Cookery first published 1759
This extract published in Penguin Books 2011
1

All rights reserved

Set in 10.75/13 pt Berkeley Oldstyle Book
Typeset by Jouve (UK), Milton Keynes
Printed in Great Britain by Clays Ltd, St Ives plc

Cover design based on a pattern from a plate from the Chelsea Porcelain Factory,
c. 1760–69. Soft-paste porcelain painted in enamels and gilt. (Photograph copyright
© Victoria & Albert Museum.) Picture research by Samantha Johnson

ISBN: 978–0–241–95087–6

www.greenpenguin.co.uk

MIX
Paper from
responsible sources
FSC™ C018179

Penguin Books is committed to a sustainable
future for our business, our readers and our
planet. This book is made from paper certified
by the Forest Stewardship Council.

Contents

Preface

From a presumption of some small success from my friends I venture to publish the following treatise. To pretend to write for fame would illy become a person in my sphere of life (who am no more than what is vulgarly called a poor publican). 'Twould be an unparalleled piece of imprudence, and wholly incompatible to reason and the nature of things. 'Twill be sufficient for me that it meets with the approbation amongst my friends and acquaintances, as may just satisfy me for the pains I have taken to collect them (though small matters) together. The chief end and design of this part of my little volume is to show, both to the experienced and unexperienced in the business, the whole and simple art of the most modern and best French Cookery; to lay down before them such an unerring guide how it may always be well managed, and please the eye as well as the taste of everybody; and to show, too, by the notorious errors I have frequently seen, how of course it must for ever fail of being either good or pleasing, and a great many favourite morsels entirely spoiled.

First, then, give me leave to advise those who please to try the following receipts, to provide a proper apparatus for the work they take in hand, without which it is impossible it can be done with the least air of decency: and before I finish this, shall further show by maxims unexceptionable, that a good dinner cannot be got up to look neat and pretty without proper utensils to work it in, such as neat stewpans of several sizes, soup-pots, &c. to do it withal, though your provisions be never so good. I have been sent for many and many a time to get dinners for some of the best families herabouts; the salute generally is: Will, (for that is my name) I want you to dress me a dinner to-day; with all my heart, Sir, says I; how many will your company be; why about ten or twelve, or thereabouts: and what would you please to have me get, Sir, for ye? O, says the gentleman, I shall leave that entirely to you; but I'll show you my larder, and you'll be the better judge how to make your bill of fare; and a vast plenty of good provisions there was, enough to make two courses, one of seven, the other of nine, with an addition only of three or four small dishes for the second course; and a fine dish of fish there was for a remove. So it was agreed that should be the thing; but, says the gentleman, be sure you make us some good things in your own way, for they are polite sort of gentry that are to dine with me. I promised my care, and wrote the bill immediately; and it was vastly approved of. My next step was to go and offer a great many compliments to Mrs. Cook about getting the dinner; and as it was her master's order I should assist her, I hoped we should agree; and the girl, I'll say that for her, returned the compliment very prettily, by saying, Sir, whatever my master or you shall order me to do, shall be done as far and as well as I am able. But Nanny (for that I found to be her name) soon got into such an air as often happens upon such occasions. Pray, Nanny, says I, where do you place your stewpans, and the other things you make use of in the cooking way? La, Sir, says she, that is all we have (pointing to one poor solitary stewpan, as one might call it,) but no more fit for the use than a wooden hand-dish. Ump, says I to myself, how's this to be? A surgeon may as well attempt to make an incision with a pair of sheers, or open a vein with an oyster-knife, as for me to pretend to get this dinner without proper tools to do it; here's neither stewpan, soup-pot, or any one thing else that is useful; there's what they call a frying-pan indeed, but black as my hat, and a handle long enough to obstruct half the passage of the kitchen. However, upon a little pause I sent away post haste for my own kitchen furniture. In the meantime Nanny and I kept on in preparing what we could, that no time might be lost. When the things came we at it again, and all was in a tolerable way, and forward enough for the time of day; but at length wanting a sieve I begg'd of Nanny to give me one, and so she did in a moment; but such a one! – I put my fingers to it and found it gravelly. Nanny, says I, this won't do, it is sandy: she look'd at it, and angry enough she was: rot our Sue, says she, she's always taking my sieve to sand her nasty dirty stairs. But, however, to be a little cleanly Nanny gave it a good thump upon the table, much about the part of it where the meat is generally laid, and whips it into the boiler where I suppose the pork and cabbage was boiling for the family, gives it a sort of a rinse, and gave it me again, with as much of the pork fat about it as would poison the whole dinner; so I said no more, but could not use it, and made use of a napkin that I slily made friends with her fellow-servant for; at which she leer'd round and set off; but I heard her say as she flirted her tail into the scullery, hang these men cooks, they are so confounded nice. – I'll be whipt, says she, if there was more sand in the sieve than would lay upon a sixpence. However, she came again presently, and I soon coax'd her into good humour again; come, says I, Nanny, I'm going to make a fricasee of chickens, observe how I cut 'em (for I'll show ye how to do any part of the dinner), and she seemed very attentive. When I had cut mine, there, says I, do you take that, and cut it in the same manner: and indeed the girl handled her knife well, and did it very prettily: then I gave her directions how to proceed; and it was done neatly, notwithstanding the story of the sandy sieve. I then took in hand to show her in what manner it was to be finished for the table. And now, dinner being dish'd up, Nanny was vastly pleased, and said, that in her judgment it was the prettiest and best she had ever seen. When 'twas over, the gentleman desired, if I had time in the evening, he should be glad I would come and get him two or three little matters for supper, for they all stay: and be sure, says he, make us just such another fricasee, for it was highly approved on; so I went and told Nanny she should do it; which was agreed to: but, Sir, says she, if I don't do right I hope you'll tell me. But it was done to my mind, and Nanny was now the cook; supper was sent in, and great praises ran from plate to plate, and they unanimously agreed that that fricasee was better than what they had for dinner. Before supper was well over out comes the gentleman to me. Will, says he, we hope you have this dish in the book you are going to publish. Yes, Sir, says I, and everything else you had to-day drest in the foreign way. But, Sir, says I, your cook did that you had for supper. My maid do it, says he, and away he went to his company. Nanny was immediately sent for, and after some questions something was given her for the care she had taken; so I wished the family a good night, and went home. The next day, just as I had finished the transcribing my first sheet for the press, in comes an elderly gentleman, a friend of mine, and took it up to read. While I was writing on he interrupted me, by asking what was meant by apparatus, here, this word says he, (holding it to me to read). Why, Sir, says I, it comprehends all necessary and useful things for dressing a dinner fit to serve a gentleman's table, particularly your pretty little made dishes, (what are generally called French dishes). Ump, says my old friend, I seldom eat any thing more than a mutton chop, or so; but, however, 'tis all very well for them that like it. Well, but Sir, says I, please to give me leave; I take it you must have a good handsome kitchen in your great house, and well furnished I suppose. Not a jot, says my good friend, not a jot, I want none. Why, Sir, says I, gentlemen in general are as well pleased with the handsome decorations of their kitchen (though they never dress a morsel of victuals there) as they are with an expensive and fine furnished parlour. Well, says he, I like your scheme very well; but what must I get? So I named several things, and their uses. Well, I'll go and see, says he, and away he went cock-a-hoop to the brazier's immediately, and buys much about as much as is necessary for the getting up such a dinner as I sent to table yesterday; which is enough for any private gentleman's family, or the best inn or tavern in England; and costs but a trifle, (for I had seen it without the old gentleman's knowing it). But in he comes to tell me what he had done, and seemed mightily pleased that I approved on't, and invited me to come to see it to-morrow. Next day I went, and was had into the kitchen by my old friend, and very neat and decent it look'd; but when I had gazed round a little, talking of his admirable taste of placing his furniture, I missed one material article, which put me in mind of an observation I have made, and often seen in small country houses; you may be sure to find a mantelpiece with spits, a hold-fast, basting-ladle, drudging-box, iron skewers, &c., but you may look all over the house and find no jack; just such is the case of my good neighbour Hackum, he seems so delighted with his new show that he lives in the kitchen, and chuses it rather than his parlour, but has not thought one word of a stove; so I addressed myself to him, while walking round by way of pleasing him, I presume, Sir, your stoves are in your back kitchen, in the old fashion way; stoves, says he, what d'ye mean by stoves? Why, Sir, little round machines of iron fix'd in brickwork about three feet from the ground, where charcoal is always burnt on all occasions in the cooking way, without which all your other materials are of no sort of use but as you see 'em now. Oh no; says he, it mayn't be often I shall invite my friends, and when I do my maid can do it all very well over this fire. (Now the fire-place, to save coals, is reduced to about the size of a salt-box.) After a little more chat about indifferent things I bid the old gentleman good-morrow, and trudged home; but dare say I shall hear from him again about the stoves, and some other little matters there must be added to it that will surprize him again, but all not worth naming. As I said so it happened, for the old man was close at my heels, and without ceremony of any sort, Will, says he, I'll have my stoves put up to-morrow, and next day I'll invite a few friends to try how my furniture answers; you'll come and dress my dinner for me, won't you? Yes, Sir, with a vast deal of pleasure. Well, says he, there will be about four of us, three of which was with him, I think, an attorney's clerk, a taylor, and a journeyman perriwig-maker, who, I suppose, are much about as great epicures as himself. What do you please I should get you, Sir, says I? Why, um, says he, I don't know, I think I have heard you talk of five and five, and a remove. Now, says he, I should think three and three and two removes would be better. (Ay, says I to myself, put two fresh dishes upon the table, and leave one tore all to pieces to keep up the symmetry of it.) Just as you like, Sir, says I, and for novelty-sake so 'tis to be. Now he ordered me to provide just what I thought proper; only that he should be glad of a soup-maigre; and then set off. Now I heard him say to his cronies, as he went along, I know I shall like that soup-maigre because they always stuff it full of meat. Maigre, says he, I suppose is French for meat; so in English we may call it a meat-soup. I went to market next morning, and provided what I judged necessary for their dinners, and took care to get enough; for I supposed 'em to be good trenchermen; and about one o'clock dinner went up, the soup, three fowls and bacon, and a large shoulder of mutton. The soup they eat all up, which was a very large old-fashioned pewter dish full; then fell aboard of the fowls, and demolished them, and so on to the mutton; but before they had finished it a dispute arose about what meat the soup was made of. Beef and bacon to be sure, says my old friend (and kept on eating like a ploughman). His right-hand man said he thought it was composed of rumps and burs.* He at the bottom took it to be made of a leg of mutton and turnips. Well, Sir, says he, to one upon the left, what think you of it? Why, Sir, I won't think of it at all: if I do I shall be sick, for I have eat too much of it. At length they sent for me, and I decided it; which surprized them. There was no other ingredients than about six carrots, as many turnips, and onions and herbs boiled to a sort of porridge, and strained through a cullender to a large quantity of toasted bread: the next three things were a hare, a turkey, (both baked, and spoiled, for want of a proper fire in the kitchen) and a plumb-pudding. There was no ceremony for clean plates; but at it they went, just as they do at one of our country club-feasts; the turkey was stript in a minute, and the poor hare tore all to pieces, (for there was not a carver amongst them) and a most profound silence there was for a long time, except only a very pretty concert of growling, smacking their chaps, and cracking of crusts: when all was over with meat, plates were called for the pudding, which disappeared in about three minutes, though no small one. The two removes, as the old gentleman called them,

* Rumps and burs are the tails flea'd, and roots of the ears of a bullock; common perquisite of a journeyman-butcher, or tanner.

were then brought in, and the question was which should be taken off? The empty dish, says one; and that they all agreed to. Take away the turkey, says the tonsor. No, says another, the hare; so as they could not agree, a third took the hare and plunged it into the turkey's dish. The removes were then put on; and that the beauty of the third course (as I call it) might be kept up, at each end was a sort of pudding, and in the middle the gibbet of the hare, and the skeleton of the turkey. Now the two puddings (improperly called so) were made as follows: I took a few potatoes boiled, and thump'd to pieces, with an egg or two, and a little sugar, for one; the other was a few old mackeroons I had in my house perhaps twenty years: I soak'd 'em well, and put them into a little milk and flour, instead of cream and eggs, seasoned it high with plenty of onions, &c., to which I added a large clove of garlick, which is enough for the dishes of a fifty-cover table served twice over, and covered it over with some good old Cheshire cheese instead of Parmesan; so that the colours were alike, and sent up, as said before. Well, neighbour, says the old gentleman, now for a bit of pudding, and then we shall have done pretty well, I hope: let's see, here's eight of us; so they were cut into so many parts, and every one took his share, and heartily they fell to, except one whose taste was not quite so depraved as the rest; he tasted, but went no farther. You don't eat, neighbour, says the opposite gentleman. I don't love sweet things, says he. Well, I do, says one that was gobbling down the highest dish that ever was. They vastly commended it, and swallowed it all down; but the beauty of it was, the mackeroon eaters eat it for a custard, and to this moment call it the best they ever tasted. But one of 'em said it had a terrible twang of a bad egg, though there was neither egg or butter in it. Well, says my old friend, with such a sort of a groan as may frequently be heard in large peals at your great feasts in and about the metropolis of this kingdom. I say, I hope every body has made a good dinner; but we may thank you for it, Mr. Cook, says he, turning to me; why we should have cut but a sad figure to-day, if we had not had the apparatusses. Pray, Sir, says one of the most learned, what is an apparatus? Why, says my old friend, laughing at him, why a stewpan is one, a pot is another, a ladle another, and many other things down in my kitchen are called apparatusses; so I left them in the midst of their sublime chat, and went home, where, to my no great surprize, I found the gentleman whose dinner I dress'd t'other day. Will, says he, why here you have made a strange racket at our house. My maid talks of nothing but you; what a pretty dinner you sent to table, and so easy, that it seemed no more trouble to ye than for her to make a Welch rabbit; but says, that if she had such a set of kitchen goods as yours, and a little of your instructions, she could do it all very well. Well, Sir, says I, if you please to furnish such things as are wanting, and spare a little of her time to peruse what I am about to publish, I make no doubt but she'll make an excellent cook. The girl is in the right on't, she told me she was afraid you would set her a spel by and by, by ordering just such another dinner, and I am sure it is impossible two made dishes can be well done with what your kitchen affords. What must I do then, says he, Will? Why has not your good old neighbour Hackum invited ye to see his kitchen since he has furnished it? No, says he. Well, he has got all quite new from top to bottom; such a set as will just do for you; and I'll tell you what it is, and then shall draw to a conclusion; but must ask the favour of one small digression. – I promised at the beginning to fix one never-erring chart to steer by, so that the weakest capacity shall never do amiss, though he mayn't arrive at once to that pitch of perfection equal to that of the celebrated Mons. Clouet. First then, my brethren, take care to begin your work betimes. Your broth and gravy for your soups and sauces should be the first thing in hand: your little matters in the pastry way may be done whilst that is going on; next prepare your fowls, collops, cutlets, or whatever it may be; put them upon plates, and range them in neat order upon the dresser before ye; next see that your meat and roast in the English way be all cleverly trimmed, trussed and singed, and ready for the spit. In like manner get all your garden things cut, pared, pick'd, and washed out into a cullender; and amongst the rest be sure you provide a plate of green onions, shallots, parsley, minced very fine, pepper and salt always ready mixed, and your spice-box always at hand; so that every thing you want may be ready at a moment's call, and not to be hunting after such trifles when your dinner should be ready to send to table. When your stewpans, &c., make their appearance, place them all in proper arrangement, and you cannot easily err. (For want of this steady care I have known a whole course stopt, and the half of a very grand dinner in a fair way of being spoiled by misplacing only one stewpan, and the cooks (though great ones) were forced to make shift with any thing they could throw together to make a dish to fill the chasm on the table; but it was found out at last that the poor scullery woman finding it among the foul things without looking under the cover, soust it into the dishkeeler, and 'twas lost. It was only a charming dish of green morels, in the room of which was served six or eight heads of celery flung into a frying-pan for a little colour, and dished up with a little sugar sifted over it.) What I observed before this long parenthesis I call good management, and will always succeed; the reverse of it is bad. I have known the time more than once or twice, that a cook has loitered away his time in the morning, and began his work perhaps at ten o'clock, and then at the wrong end too: so that time has so elapsed upon his hands that it was impossible for him to be ready at the hour set for sending to table; so that instead of winning the praises of his master or lady, and the rest of the good company, he gets into disgrace, and loses his character. This is what is meant by saying the cook can never do well, for they must fail of it if they are regardless of time, so take it by the forelocks, my friends, and follow the instructions in the treatise before ye, and you'll be sure to be right, and soon procure to yourself a vast deal of fame. Now, Sir, please to give me leave to make a catalogue of such things as you stand in need of in your kitchen: Two little boilers, one big enough for your broth or boiling a leg of mutton, and the other for the boiling of a couple of fowls or so, a soup-pot, eight small stewpans of different sizes, two very large ones, and covers to them all, a neat handy frying pan that may serve as well for frying any little matters, as an amlette or pancakes, a couple of copper ladles, two or three large copper spoons, a slice or two, and an egg spoon, all tinn'd; a pewter cullender, three or four sieves, (one of lawn); to which you may add half a dozen copper cups that hold about three-fourths of half a pint, and as many of a lesser size, and an *etamine or two for the straining your thick soups, cullies or creams. Your cook will find uses for all these utensils, if you should ever give an order to get the dishes prescribed in the following receipts: but all your wooden ladles, skimmers, cabbage-nets, and such nasty things, banish them from your kitchen, let them not touch your broth, soup, fish, or any thing else; keep nothing of that sort there but two or three large wooden spoons, and them always kept clean for their particular uses, such as stirring any of your sauces in your stewpans, for pewter will melt, and copper will fret the tinning off. It is needless to say any thing of little round sauce-pans for venison sauce, warming of gravy, melting of butter or fish sauce, or the like. 'Tis supposed every house has a provision of that sort. And now let my brother or sister cook come on clean and neat like my friend and patron Clouet, with two or three clean aprons and rubbers, and follow the rules laid down in the easy method prescribed in the following receipts; and if it is not the most egregious blunderer in the world I'll be answerable for all that is done amiss. What my friend Clouet will say when he hears of this rash adventure of

* An etamine is a fluff made on purpose for these uses, and are sold at many shops in London.

mine I cannot guess; but this I'm sure of, he'll be my voucher that it is all authentic.

As to the character of that gentleman, much at this time must not be said: that he was an honest man I verily believe, and might I have leave to give him praise equal to his merit, I would venture to say he was worthy of the place he enjoyed in that noble family he had the honour to live in. Much has been said of his extravagance, but I beg pardon for saying it, he was not that at all, nay, so far from it, this I can aver, that setting aside the two soups, fish, and about five *gros entrees* (as the French call them) he has, with the help of a couple of rabbits or chickens, and six pigeons, completed a table of twenty-one dishes at a course, with such things as used to serve only for garnish round a lump of great heavy dishes before he came here, such as calves and lambs' sweetbreads, sheep and lambs' rumps, turkeys' livers, and many other such like things, of which, with proper sauces, he used to make as many pretty neat dishes. The second or third great dinner he drest for my Lord Duke, he ordered five calves' heads to be brought in, which made us think some extravagant thing was on foot, but we soon saw it was just the reverse of it; he made five very handsome and good dishes of what he took, and the heads not worth a groat less each. The tongues, pallets, eyes, brains, and ears. The story of his *affiette* of popes-eyes, the quintessence of a ham for sauce, and the gravy of twenty-two partridges for sauce for a brace, was always beyond the credit of any sensible person; so shall leave that untouch'd. The second course dishes, or *extremes*, he made as much difference in,

I mean as to the expence, for what formerly (and that since my time too) made but one of most of them, he made two, and all prettier, because they were not so heavy. But I am afraid I shall launch out too far in encomiums on my friend Clouet; but beg to be excused by all my readers. One thing more and then I'll leave him to his new master marshal Richlieu (for there I am informed he now lives as steward, or *maitre d'hotel*). That I thought him very honest I think I said before, not only that, but he was of a temper so affable and agreeable, as to make every body happy about him. He would converse about indifferent matters with me or his kitchen boy, and the next moment, by a sweet turn in his discourse, give pleasure by his good behaviour and genteel deportment, to the first steward in the family. His conversation is always modest enough; and having read a little he never wanted something to say, let the topick be what it would.

Soups

Before we begin with Mr. Clouet's method or art of making his potages or soups, 'tis necessary first of all to point out his manner of preparing his bouillion or broth. Instead of the leg or shin of beef (which are the common pieces in your two-penny cut shops) take eight or ten pounds of the lean part, which, in London, is called the mouse-buttock, with a little knuckle of veal, neatly trimm'd, that it may serve to send up in your soup. A pot that holds three or four gallons will do. When you have wash'd your meat put it over the stove full of water; take care that 'tis well skimmed before it boils, or you'll lose the whole beauty of your soups and sauces; sprinkle in a little salt now and then, and 'twill cause the skim to rise; let it but just boil upon the stove, but take it off, and to simmer sideways, then all the soil will sink to the bottom; to season it take ten or twelve large sound onions, eight or ten whole carrots, three or four turnips, a parsnip, two or three leeks, and a little bundle of celery tied up, a few cloves, a blade or two of mace, and some whole white pepper; let it boil no longer than the meat is thoroughly boiled to eat; for to boil it to rags (as is the common practice) it makes the broth thick and grouty, and spoils the pleasing aspect of all your dinner, and hurts the meat that thousands of families would leap mast-high at; strain it through a lawn sieve into a clean

1

earthen pan, skim the fat all off, and make your soups and gravies, &c., of it as you have directions in the following receipts. N.B. Mons. Clouet never made use of either thyme, marjoram, or savoury in any of his soups or sauces, except in some few made dishes, as you'll see in going on; and where carrots are used be sure to cut off the rind, or 'twill give a reddish hue, which is disagreeable in any thing. This recipe of making my broth takes up a pretty deal of room; but as all the rest depends upon this being well done, 'tis of the utmost consequence to see that 'tis so. You may wonder of what use so many roots, &c., can be of; my answer is, you can make no savoury dish good without them. In this the French always were too cunning for us. The best of them all will not pretend to do any thing for the best gentleman in the kingdom, unless they could be allowed plenty of every thing from the garden. No, no. *Point des lesgumes; point de Cuisiniere.* No good garden things, no French cook. And from my own experience I know it to be so. I would venture myself to make a better soup with two pounds of meat, and such garden things as I liked, than is made of eight pound for the tables of most of our gentry, and all for want of better knowing the uses of roots and other vegetables. And now, my good cook, take care that this is well done; 'tis by this as 'tis by your *Aqua Fontana* in an apothecary's shop, scarce any thing can be done and finished well without it. After this I shall endeavour to be much more concise. I shall say nothing of drawing and trussing of fowls, and singing,*

* i.e. singeing. (Ed.)

peeling, scraping, picking, or washing of garden things, trimming of your meats, scaling or cleaning of fish, or any thing of that sort, for so much tautology would fill up a volume half as big as what I propose this to be, but shall put down the composition in as few words as it will admit of. – Next then –

TO MAKE A CLEAR GRAVY OF VEAL FOR SOUP.

Three or four pound of a leg of veal, a slice of raw ham, in the middle of a stewpan, with a morsel of fat bacon under it, two or three onions, carrots, and some parsley upon it, pour in two or three spoonfuls of your broth, cover it close, set it upon a slow fire till it becomes dry and brown; but you must observe that that part of the pan that is uncovered with meat will take colour first, so that you must often move it round, that it may every part be of an equal brownness; and if you nick the time between its being of a nice brown and burning, put in your broth – full as many quarts as there is pounds of meat, let it simmer for half an hour or a little more, strain it through a lawn sieve; and if you have taken care you will find it of a fine colour, and clear as rock-water, and may use of it for any sort of gravy-soup or sauce.

POTAGE DE SANTE AUX HERBES.
Soup sante with herbs.

Of herbs or vegetables you must shift with celery and endives in the winter, but add a lettuce if you can get it;

provide a duckling, or a chicken neatly blanch't, and boil it in your soup, which is nothing more than the same broth and gravy as before. With the celery, &c., cut in bits about an inch long; let it boil gently for an hour or so, and when 'tis almost your time of dining add a little spinage, sorrel, and chervil, chopt but not small, and boil it about five minutes; prepare your crusts as before in a stewpan, and lay at the bottom of your dish, lay your duckling in the middle, and pour your soup over it, and serve it up with some thin bits of celery for garnish, or without, as you like best.

For the summer season you may add a handful of young pease, heads of asparagus or sparagrass, nice little firm bits of cauliflower, bottoms of artichokes, and many other things that the season affords; 'tis but altering the name from one to the other, as you make your bills of fare daily; and you make twenty soups by this one receipt as easy as one; for instance, *Soup sante aux petit pois*, i.e. with young pease; so on to the rest.

POTAGE, OR SOUP A LA JULIENNE.

This is a favourite soup, and now highly in vogue, and not much more expensive than the former. Instead of beef and veal for its broth, make it of a hen and veal and a bit of ham, seasoned as before. Make your gravy of it as for *Soup sante*; provide some bits of carrots about an inch in length, cut longways, slice it very thin, and cut it into small square pieces the full length; prepare some turnips in the same manner, some celery in the smallest bits you can of equal length; blanch all this two or three minutes, strain them, and put them in your soup-pot, and when your gravy is ready strain it to them; add to this a little purslane, the hearts of two or three lettuce, a little chervil, spinage, and sorrel, minced fine, and boil it together gently for an hour; get your crusts ready as before, and serve it up. If green pease are to be had fling in a handful or two, but very young, for old ones will thicken your soup, and make it have a bad look. You may serve a chicken up in it, or veal as before.

POTAGE A LA REINE. – WHAT QUEEN I KNOW NOT.

To make a proper stock for this, to about three quarts of broth put about a pound of lean veal and some bits of ham, two or three whole onions, carrots, parsley, and a blade of mace; boil it all together as you do gravy, for an hour; take all from your broth, and stir in the white part of a roasted fowl or chicken, and about two ounces of sweet almonds blanch'd, and both well pounded, the yolks of three or four hard eggs mash'd, with the soft of a manchet boiled in good milk or cream; rub it well through an etamine, and pour it into your soup-pot; take care to keep it boiling hot, but never let it boil a moment over your stove, but keep it moving; provide some crusts well soak'd, and a chicken in your dish, and serve it up, with a little of your best gravy poured in circles or patches. This is the most modern way.

Another fashion I have often seen, and I think no bad one where plate is used: put your soak'd bread into your dish, and set on a chaffing-dish of charcoal, so that it boil to cleave to the bottom; but take care you don't let it burn: and yet it ought to be pretty brown, and should be scraped off with the soup-spoon. No other difference but that.

POTAGE AUX NANTILES;
OR, NANTILE SOUP.

Nantiles are a sort of grain that come from abroad, and are sold at most of the oil-shops in London, in shape like a vetch or tare, but much less. Take about a quart of them, and boil in water only till very tender, for your stock. You must be so extravagant as to have a roasted partridge; pick off the flesh, and I'll presently shew the use of it: the bones you may crush to pieces, and put to them some bits of ham, with about three quarts of broth and gravy mix'd: add to it as before onions and carrots and parsley; boil this as the last; take all from it; see that your partridge meat is well pounded, and your nantiles, and stir them into your broth, and let boil a few minutes; strain it through your etamine, and serve it with a partridge in the middle, and some thin morsels of bacon for garnish, which may be both boil'd in your broth, being well blanch'd; have some crusts soak'd as before, and serve it up.

POTAGE A LA PUREE VERTE
Pease Soup.

If you make this soup in the season of green-pease, take about three pints of old ones, boil them tender, and pound 'em well, a bit of butter in a large stewpan, and fry, with some bits of ham, two or three carrots, onions, turnips, and a parsnip, a leek or two, some bits of celery, and mint-tops, a little spice and whole pepper; pour in about three quarts of broth, and boil it an hour; take all out, and put in your pease, with the soft of a French roll well soak'd in a little broth, for pease will not thicken enough at this time of the year; set it over your fire a few minutes, and pass it through your etamine; provide a little celery and endives, or lettuce ready boiled, with a few young pease; put them to your soup, and let it simmer till dinner-time; add a little handful of spinage and sorrel chop'd, which may boil five minutes; prepare your crusts as before, and serve it up with a square bit of bacon cut in bits through the rind, and may be boiled with your broth.

For the winter season make use of blue pease, which are always to be had in London, and celery and endives to serve up in it; and stain it with the juice of spinage.

UN PLAT DE SOUP POUR SOUPER.
Soup for Supper.

This may seem to be but a simple thing to place among these high matters; but I never see it come from table without a terrible wound in it. If it has but the approbation of few it will pay very well for the room it takes up here.

To a quart of good new milk put a pint of cream, a bit of lemon-peel, a laurel-leaf or two, and a stick of cinnamon, and a few coriander seeds, and some good sugar;

boil it for a few minutes, and set off to cool; blanch two ounces of sweet almonds, with two or three bitter ones, pound them with a drop of water to a paste, and stir them in your milk, rub it through an etamine, pour it back into your stewpan, and make it just boiling. Provide the yolks of about ten eggs, and pour in beat nice and smooth, stir it upon your stove carefully for a minute or two, and it is ready to serve to table, putting on it some rusks or toasts of French bread.

WATER SOUCHY.

This is rather a Dutch dish, and for change no bad one. To make this in perfection you should have several sorts of small fish, flounders, gudgeons, eels, perch, and a pike or two; but it is often with perch only; they ought to be very fresh; take care all is very clean, for what they are boiled in is the soup; cut little notches in all, and put them a little while in fresh spring water; (this is what is called crimping of fish in London); put them into a stewpan with as much water as you think will fill your dish, half a pint of white wine, a spoonful or two of vinegar, and as much salt as you would for broth. Put them over your fire in cold water, and take particular care you skim it well in boiling; provide some parsley roots cut in slices, and boiled very tender, and a large quantity of leaves of parsley boiled nice and green. When your fish have boiled gently for a quarter of an hour take them from the fire, and put in your roots, and when you serve it to table strew your leaves over it; take care not to break your fish, and pour your liquor on softly and hot; some plates of bread and butter are generally served up with this, so be sure to have them ready.

POTAGE MAIGRE AUX HERBES.
Herb soup without meat.

For the summer season three or four carrots, a little bunch of green onions, a few beet-leaves, and a handful of spinage and sorrel, a little purslane and chervil, and two or three lettuce, and some spice and pepper, strip all into small bits and fry them in a large stewpan, with a bit of fresh butter; pour in about two quarts of water, and let it boil gently for an hour at least, strain it off to the soft of a French roll well soaked, and pass it through your etamine; prepare the heart of two of nice light savoys or cabbage, a couple of lettuce, and a handful or two of young pease, stew them well, and drain them upon a sieve; when it draws towards your dinner-time have ready the yolks of half a dozen eggs, mixed well with half a pint of cream; put your pease, &c. into the soup, and boil it for a few minutes, a few slices of white bread, then your cream and eggs; stir it well together, cover it down very close till you are ready for it, just shew it to the fire and send it up. This soup is frequently done with cucumbers quartered, and the seed cut out, instead of the things before-mentioned. For the winter, celery and endives, white beet-roots, sliced thin, or the bottoms of artichokes, which in some families are preserved for such uses, and in most of the oil-shops in and about London.

Fish

Fish being the second first course dish takes its place next.

    N.B. Mr. Clouet never boiled any fish of any sort in the plain way; and as almost every body knows the easy method of dressing of them so, and their proper sauces, 'twill be needless to put it down here. I propose but four for his *gros entrees*, or removes, which is a turbot, salmon, a pike, and carps, done in manner following.

TURBOT A L'ITALIENNE.
Turbot in the Italian way.

Cut the fins and tail of your fish off, and lay to soak in a marinade for an hour or two, which is a little vinegar, white wine, salt and water, some green onions and bay leaves, with some blades of mace and whole pepper; take your fish and dry it upon a cloth, and place it in a stewpan just its size. The most common sauce in Mr. Clouet's way was that at top, *sauce Italienne*; to make which, with about a pint of good gravy, put a glass or two of Rhenish, two or three spoonfuls of oil, the juice of a couple of lemons, an anchovy or two, a little pepper and salt, some shallots minced very fine, and a little bundle of green onions and parsley tied up, pour it on your fish, so much as will just cover it; if you find this not quite enough add a spoonful or two of your cullis [p. 15], cover it down very close, and set it upon a slow stove to simmer very gently for about an hour, that it may be done rather by fumigation than hasty boiling; take a large ladle of your cullis and strain to it, about as much of your liquor from your fish, add a few olives pared from the kernel, or capers; dish your fish up hot, boil your sauce a few minutes and pour it over it, strewing a little parsley minced very fine over, and garnish with a great deal of whole, fresh and fine pick'd.

This is an excellent way to dress a John o'Dorey, or upon a pinch a large plaice is no bad thing.

SAUMON AUX CREVETTES.
Salmon with shrimp sauce.

Of a salmon the jowl is preferr'd to any other part; notch it to the bone on both sides about an inch apart; lay it in a marinade, as before mentioned; put it into some long stewpan just its bigness if you can, with a fish plate or napkin under it, that you may take it out without breaking; put to it a pint of white wine, a dash of vinegar, some sweet basil and thyme, whole pepper, salt and mace, two or three shallots, a bunch of parsley and green onions; pour in as much water as will just cover it, let your lid be shut close upon it, and about an hour before your dinner put it over a slow stove to simmer, and prepare your sauce as follows: provide as many small prawns or shrimps (the tails only) as you think necessary for your piece of salmon; put into your stewpan to them a proportionate quantity of cullis, add to it a little basil, pimpernel, thyme and parsley, all minced very fine, with a dash of white wine; boil all about a quarter of an hour, squeeze in the juice of a lemon or two, take care that the fish is well drained, and put meat into your dish, pour your sauce over, and serve it up; garnish with lemons cut in quarters.

Trouts may be done in the same manner.

At times when *maigre sauces* are chosen, make a little broth of a few small fish, season as above, skim it well, and boil it but about half an hour, strain it into a stewpan, add a bit of butter mix'd with some fine flour, provide the yolks of four or five eggs, and about a gill of cream; stir your butter, &c. to prevent its being lumpy, and let it boil a little while, set it off the fire, put in your prawns with your cream and eggs,* cover it close for a few minutes, keep it moving over the stove for a moment, squeeze in your lemon, and serve it up.

Such a sauce as this may serve for any sort of fish, either stew'd or boil'd; and without the help of Mr. Clouet, I have many a time toss'd up a dish of fish with only its own natural broth seasoned in the manner prescribed; I mean by stewing and straining its broth, and thickened as above.

* Note that the cream and eggs are not boiled but put in after the boiling. (Ed.)

UN BROCHET FARCEZ,
SAUCE AUX CAPERS.
Pike with force-meat and caper sauce.

Prepare your pike thus: gut it without cutting of it open, but take care it is well cleaned; cut a notch down the back from head to tail, turn it round, and fasten the tail in the mouth, and lay it in a marinade as before: for your farce or forcemeat take the udder of a leg of veal, or the kidney part of a loin of lamb, some fat bacon cut in dice, the spawn or melt of the fish, some green onions, a mushroom or two, or truffles, parsley, and salt, a little nutmeg and pepper, add a morsel of butter to fry it, chop it all well, and the soft of a French roll soak'd in cream or milk, pound all together in a large mortar, with three or four eggs; try if it is seasoned to your mind, and fill the belly of your fish, and close up that part that is cut in the back; make it nice and even; take two or three eggs, daub it well over, and strew some crumbs of bread upon it, and bake it in a gentle oven, the time according to the bigness of your pike. For your sauce, to two or three ladles of your cullis add two or three large spoonfuls of whole capers, some parsley minced fine, the juice of two lemons, a little minced shallot, and serve it up in your dish hot, but not poured over.

As this dish is bak'd, garnish with a large quantity of fry'd parsley.

The French are fond of barbel, chubs, or chevins, done in the same manner.

DES CARPES A LA COUR.
Carps done the court fashion.

A brace of carp is handsomest for a dish. Place your fish in a stewpan that they just fill, upon two or three slices of bacon or ham, that you may turn them the easier; pour in as much wine as will just cover them, a ladle or two of cullis, season with a bunch of onions and parsley, some cloves and mace, pepper, salt, and three or four bay leaves, and two or three shallots and mushrooms, an anchovy or two; and let your melts or soft rowes stew with the fish about half an hour; but the spawn or hard rowes boil separate, and when your sauce is ready cut it in pieces, and put in, for it is very apt to crumble to bits and spoil the comeliness of it. For the sauce take about half of what the fish are stewed in, and as much cullis added to it. For a *sauce hachee*, a little burnet, pimpernel, a mushroom or two, and some parsley, all minced very fine; take your melts or spawns and cut in small pieces, and boil a little while in your sauce; dish up your fish, add the juice of a lemon, and pour hot upon 'em; garnish with parsley only.

Tench may be done just in the same manner.

Gros Entrees of Meat

I propose to put twelve *gros entrees* of meat; but first of all to shew Mr. Clouet's method of preparing his coulis or cullis.

Take a stewpan that will hold about four quarts, put a thin slice or two of bacon at the bottom, about two pound of veal, a piece of ham, three or four carrots, onions and parsley, with a head or two of celery, pour in about a pint of your broth, cover it close, and let it go gently on upon a slow stove for an hour; when it comes to be almost dry watch it narrowly, so as to bring it to a nice brown, fill it up with broth, and let it boil softly about half an hour; take about half a pound of fresh butter, melt it, three or four large spoonfuls of fine flour, and rub over a stove till it is a fine yellowish or light-brown colour, pour it into your gravy, and stir it well after boiling ten minutes or so; take your meat and roots out, and pass it through your etamine;* take off the fat, and set it handy for such uses as you'll find in the following receipts. Be sure great care is taken of this, for on it the goodness and beauty of all the rest depends.

* Sieve of thin cloth, like muslin. (Ed.)

LONGE DE VEAU MARINEE, SAUCE BRUNE.
Loin of veal marinaded, with a brown sauce.

Your loin of veal should be put into the marinade the day before; take about two quarts of new milk, and put to it some green onions, a shallot or two, parsley, a little spice, whole pepper, salt, two or three bay leaves, and some coriander seed; put your veal in, and keep it well turned so as to soak it well, till it should be spitted next day, cover it with paper with butter rubb'd on it, and roast it gently till it is well done. I have known a cook baste with this marinade, but Mr. Clouet never, nor with any thing else. For your sauce, mix about a pint of your cullis thinned with a little gravy, mince two or three mushrooms and capers, a little parsley, and a shallot or two, pour it into your dish, adding the juice of a lemon, with the kidney undermost.

UN JAMBON AUX EPINARS.
Ham with spinage.

In this the French beat us again. You scarce see a ham go to table fit to eat in the English way. We serve it up generally not half soak'd, salt as brine, and almost as hard as a flint, and our sauce most times nothing more than a little greasy cabbage and melted butter, and sometimes for garnish an ugly fowl or two, or half a dozen pigeons badly trussed. The French go another way to work; they take their ham and trim every jot of the outside off (*et mettez le tremper*) put it in soak two or three days in milk and water, and with a handful of coriander seeds; and in boiling they throw in a little white wine, and a few blades of mace, and whole pepper, a carrot or two, and an onion, which adds to the flavour and but a trifling expence; let it simmer for four or five hours, or till it is tender as a chicken; take care to preserve it whole, and make your sauce thus; stew your spinage nice and green, squeeze the juice from it quite dry, and chop it fine, put to it in a stewpan a ladle of your cullis, a little pepper, salt and nutmeg, see that it is of a good flavour and thickness, and serve it up with the juice of a lemon under your ham, with the skin taken clean off.

JAMBON ROTIS.
Roasted ham.

For this *entree* is generally provided a new Westphalia or Bayonne ham, soaked as before; put it to a slowish fire, and baste it with a little Rhenish or other white wine pretty constantly till it is done; but before you spit it draw your knife round between the fat and the sward; and in roasting you may easily take it all off; make it of a nice colour, and for your sauce dash into it a ladle or two of your cullis, a glass of Champagne or Rhenish, and a few tops of asparagus, cauliflower, or capers, add the juice of a lemon, and serve it up hot.

JIGOT DE MOUTON AUX ONIONS ESPANIOLS
Jiggot of mutton with Spanish onions.

A jiggot of mutton is the leg with part of the loin; provide such a one as has been killed two or three days at least, thump it well, and bind it with packthread, that you keep whole when you take it out; put it into a pot about its bigness, and pour in a little of your broth, and cover it with water; put in about a dozen of Spanish onions, with the rinds on, three or four carrots, a turnip or two, some parsley, and any other herbs you like; cover down close, and stew it gently for three or four hours; but take your onions after an hour's stewing, and take the first and second rinds off, put 'em into a stewpan, with a ladle or two of your cullis, a mushroom or two, or truffles minced, and a little parsley; take your mutton and drain clean from the fat and liquor; make your sauce hot, and well seasoned, squeeze in a lemon, and serve it up with the onions round it, and pour the sauce over it.

CHINE DE MOUTON AUX CONCOMBRES, OU SAUCE HACHEE.
*Chine of mutton with cucumber sauce,
or a sauce of herbs minced.*

You must provide the two fore-quarters of mutton, small and fat; cut it down the sides, and chop thro' the shoulders and breasts, so that it may lay even in your dish, raise the skin all off without cutting or tearing; prepare *un petit salpicon des herbes*, as the French call it; i.e. scrape a little fat bacon, and take a little thyme, marjoram, savoury, parsley, three or four green onions, a mushroom or two, and a shallot, mince all very fine, and fry them gently in the bacon; add a little pepper, and when it is almost cold, with a paste-brush daub it all over the back of your meat, skewer the skin over it, spit it with three or four large skewers, and wrap some paper over it well buttered, roast it enough very gently, and for your sauce provide some cucumbers (if in season) nicely quarter'd and fry'd in a bit of butter to a brown colour; strain them upon a sieve for a minute or two, and put them into a ladle or two of your cullis, boil them a little while, and throw in some minced parsley, the juice of a lemon, and serve it up. – For your hachee, or sauce of herbs, prepare just such matters as are fry'd for the first part of it; take a stewpan, with as much of your cullis as is necessary, and strew all in, and boil about half an hour very softly; take the paper and skin of your chine, and send it to table with the sauce poured over it, adding the juice of a lemon; and taste it to try if it is well flavour'd.

The hind chine of mutton is not so commonly dressed among the French, but sometimes done in the same way.

CHINE DERNIERE DE MOUTON EN SURPRIZE A LA CLOUET
*Hind chine of mutton after the
fashion of Mr. Clouet.*

Provide a nice small fat chine not too fresh; take off the skin as the other, make a sort of paste of butter, mixt with some thyme, parsley, and a mushroom, a little pepper and salt, smear it over the back, and fillets of your meat, and skewer on the skin, spit with skewers (for nothing is more disagreeable than a spit-hole through all the meat), roast it gently with some paper over it; but take care 'tis not too much done; for it is hash'd in the manner following; raise the skin so as to preserve it whole, and cut the fillets out from end to end, and those of the inside, and save all its gravy; keep your bones hot before the fire, and cut your fillets ten times thinner than a wafer if it's possible; put to it a ladle or two of your cullis, with the gravy, a shallot or two minced, and some minced parsley, toss it up over a stove till 'tis boiling hot, but don't boil it a minute, squeeze in a lemon, dish up your chine, pouring the hash over it, and cover it with the skin neatly, and send it up.

With a great deal of care a shoulder of mutton may be done in the same manner. These are dishes that never fail of being well eaten.

ROTS BOEUF, D'AGNEAU, OU DEUX QUARTIERS D'AGNEAUX DERRIERE, AUX EPINARS A LA CREME.
Two hind-quarters of lamb, with spinage.

Take your two quarters of lamb, truss your knuckles in nicely, and lay it in soak two or three hours in some milk, coriander seed, a little salt, two or three onions and parsley; put it boiling in but little water, skim it well, put in some flour and water well mixt, a lemon or two pared and sliced, a bit of sewet, and a little bunch of onions and parsley, stir it well from the bottom, and boil it gently, and these ingredients will make it white as a curd; prepare your spinage as for the ham, with this difference, instead of cullis with that seasoning; put to it about a pint of cream, a bit of butter mixt with flour, a little pepper and salt and nutmeg, stir it over a slow stove till it is of a nice consistence, squeeze in the juice of a lemon, pour it into the dish, and lay your lamb upon it after draining it from fat and water, and take off any of your seasonings that may chance to hang to it.

A neck of veal is frequently done in the same way, taking the chine-bone off, and trimming it neatly.

SURLOIN DE BOEUF, FILLET HACHEE.
Surloin of beef, the fillet hash'd.

Trim your beef to look decent, and put it into a marinade the day before, as you did your veal, wrap it up in paper to roast it; take out the inside fillet, and slice it very thin; take care of your gravy, and put your meat into a stewpan with it, and as much of your cullis as is necessary to well fill the part where the meat was taken out, with some flowing in the dish; season with only pepper, salt, a shallot or two, and minced parsley; make it thorough boiling hot; add the juice of a lemon, and serve it up what we call the wrong side uppermost.

DINDON A LA BRAIZE AUX CHATAIGNES, SAUCE SALPICON.
*Turkey in a braize with chesnuts,
with a salpicon sauce.*

Lard your turkey with a few large square pieces of bacon, seasoned with a little beaten spices, pepper and salt, and a little parsley; take a pot about its bigness, and line it with thin slices of bacon, and cover with the same; season pretty high, with onions, carrots, a turnip or two, such herbs as you like, a little spice and pepper, parsley, and a head or two of celery, fill up with a little broth and water mixt, cover it down close, and let it go gently on till every part of your turkey is very tender.

N.B. This braize will serve for any thing else the same day, or for four or five days following. I should first have spoke of preparing the chesnuts by blanching, peeling, and putting into the body of the turkey, with a little farce or force-meat in the crop, and skewer'd up; let your turkey lay in the braize till towards dinner-time; and now prepare your salpicon; take a thin slice or two of boiled ham, a veal sweetbread, the yolk or two of hard eggs, or a knot is better, a pickled cucumber or two, two or three mushrooms cut all into small dice, and put into as much cullis as is suitable for your dish, dash in a glass of Champagne, or other white wine; boil all a little while, throw in a little minc'd parsley, try if it is seasoned to your mind, squeeze in the juice of a lemon, and pour over your turkey well drained, and serve it up.

A couple of large fowls done in the same manner

serves very well for a large *entree*, with the same sauce, only leave out the chesnuts.

PIECE DU BOEUF TREMBLANT.
Piece of beef trembling.

A rump of beef is the best piece for this, but it must be vastly cut and trimm'd; cut the edge of the aich-bone off quite close to the meat, that it may lay flat in your dish, and if it is large cut it at the chump end so as to make it square, hang it up for three or four days or more without salt; prepare a marinade as before, and leave it all night in soak, fillet it two or three times across, and put it into a pot, the fat uppermost, put in as much water as will a little more than cover it, take care to skim it well, and season as you would for a good broth, adding about a pint of white wine; let it simmer for as long a time as it will hang together; there are many sauces for this piece of meat; but the two favourites with Clouet were *sauce aux carrots* and *sauce hachee*; sauce with carrots, and a sauce of herbs, &c. minced. Your carrots should be cut an inch long, and boiled a little in water, and afterwards stewed in some cullis proportionate to your meat; when they are done tender, dash in a glass of white wine, a little minced shallot and parsley, and the juice of a lemon; take your beef out upon a cloth, clean it neatly from its fat and liquor, place it hot and whole in your dish, and pour your sauce hot over it, and serve it up. The *sauce hachee* you saw before. But strew some minced parsley over it, it looks prettier.

PATTEE DRESSEE DES CANARDS.
A raised duckling pye.

Take the livers of your ducklings, and make a little forcemeat with a little scraped bacon, a mushroom or two, some herbs, pepper, salt and nutmeg pounded well together, a morsel of soft bread, and an egg or two, mix it well, and put it into them, put 'em into your crust with a bunch of onions and parsley, a little pepper strewed over, and cover them with some slices of bacon, and finish your making: before you send it to table, take a little broth and cullis mixt; take out your bacon and fat, and pour in your sauce, with the juice of a lemon and serve it up without the lid. – You may add the heads of a few asparagus, or green pease, in your sauce.

PATTEE D'OISON PICQUEE.
Goose-pye larded with bacon.

Provide a young fat goose, and lard in a few pieces of bacon, seasoned with spice, pepper and salt, and some herbs; place in your crust, and sprinkle a little salt and pepper, pour in a little broth, a bunch of onions and parsley, with a little shallot, and cover it with a slice or two of bacon; bake it well, and provide a sauce as follows: take the feet, pinions, and gizzard of your goose, stew them well, put them into a stewpan with a ladle of your cullis seasoned with such matters as you have seen before; cut up your pye and pour it in; but take off the fat clean, for nothing is more disagreeable in a sauce than the oily fat of a goose, turkey, or a fowl.

Petit Entrees

The next twenty are what the French call *petits entrees*. – Dishes of a lesser size.

Four of fish, four of meats, four of pastry, four of fowls, and four others.

MATELOTTE DES CARPS.
Matelotte of carps.

Provide one large, or a brace of a smaller size, cut in seven or eight pieces, fry them in a bit of fresh butter, pour in about a pint of red wine, a ladle of gravy, tie up a bunch of green onions, herbs and parsley, a few cloves, pepper and salt, and three or four bay leaves, stew all together gently about three quarters of an hour, strain it into another stewpan to as much cullis as will do for your dish, and put your fish to it, put your bay leaves in, and a spoonful or two of capers, an anchovy chopt very fine; add the juice of a lemon and serve it up, with your melts or spawn for garnish, boiled in a little vinegar, salt and water; and have some bits of bread fry'd to stick about between your pieces of fish.

Tench and eels make an excellent dish done the same way.

FRICASEE DES ANGUILLES AU VIN DE CHAMPAGNE, OU VIN DE RHIN.
Fricasee of eels with Champagne, or Rhenish wine.

Skin three or four large eels, and notch them from end to end, cut 'em into four or five pieces each, and lay them from end to end, cut 'em into four or five pieces each, and lay them in some spring water for half an hour to crimp them, dry them in a cloth, and toss them over a fire a few minutes in a bit of fresh butter, a green onion or two, and a little parsley; but take care the colour of neither is alter'd by burning your butter; pour in about a pint of white wine, and as much good broth, pepper, salt, and a blade of mace; let it stew about as long as the carp above, and thicken it with a bit of butter and flour, prepare your *liaison* (as the French call it) with the yolks of four or five eggs beat smooth, with two or three spoonfuls of broth, grate in a little nutmeg, a little minced parsley; towards your dinner-time let your eels be boiling hot, and pour in your egg, &c., toss it over the fire for a moment, add the juice of a lemon, and serve it up. Be very cautious you don't let it curdle by keeping it too long upon the fire after the eggs are in, for if 'tis ever so good and palatable before, nobody at table will touch it, from its bad appearance.

Tench cut in pieces make a very good dish done as above.

DES SOLES FARCEZ, SAUCE
AUX FINES HERBES.
Soles with forcemeat, sauce of minced herbs.

For this provide a pair of large soles, or three or four of a lesser size, take the skin off from both sides, and soak them in a marinade, as shewn before, for an hour, dry them upon a cloth, cut them down the middle, and with the point of your knife raise up the fillets; make a little force-meat of the flesh of a couple of plaice or flounders, a morsel of the fat of veals udder or sewet, season with a mushroom or two, a green onion and parsley minced, pepper and salt and nutmeg, scrape a bit of bacon, and fry it very gently; let it cool, and pound it well with a bit of bread well soak'd and a couple of eggs, taking away one white; lift up the flesh of the soles, and crowd in as much as you can; brush some egg over them, and strew crumbs of bread, a little oil, or oil'd butter poured upon it; bake 'em about half an hour of a fine colour, and send them up garnished with some little pats of your force-meat fry'd, and some parsley. For your sauce take a little sweet basil, pimpernel, thyme and parsley, a shallot or two minced fine, with a ladle of your clear gravy, and a dash of white wine, pepper and salt; boil all together for a few minutes, squeeze in a lemon or two, and send it up in a fish sauce-boat.

Small prills are good done in this manner, or any other firm-flesh'd fish.

DES TRANCHES DE SAUMON
A LA CLOUET, SAUCE DES
ECREVISSES OU DES CREVETTES.
Salmon in slices Mr. Clouet's fashion,
with crawfish sauce, or prawns.

Take about six slices of salmon, and lay in soak in what
the French call a hot marinade; scrape some fat bacon,
or a piece of butter, and a little minced shallot, a green
onion, a mushroom, sweet basil and parsley, and a very
little pepper and salt; fry all gently for two or three minutes, and put your salmon immediately in it, and keep it
turn'd pretty often, with a few slices of lemon and a bay
leaf or two; lay it upon your grid-iron made very hot,
that you may turn it well; prepare a little cullis of prawns
or crawfish. As for the crawfish soup, stew the tails in it
a quarter of an hour, with an anchovy chopt fine; add
the juice of a lemon, dish up your fish with the sauce
pour'd over, and garnish with either of your shell-fish,
taking the shell from the tail.

Trouts make an exceeding good dish after the same
manner, only broiled whole, and cut in little notches
from eye to fork.

UN PATTEE DE POULETS AUX
FEUILLETAGES.
A chicken pye with light crust.

Cover the bottom of your dish or pattypan with a nice
light paste, cut your chickens as for a fricasee, lay them

in, and season with pepper, salt, and a bit of mace, put in a little bundle of green onions and parsley tied, a spoonful or two of broth, cover with thin slices of bacon; put your lid nicely on, and bake it about an hour and an half; before you serve it up take off the top, your bacon out, and clean well from fat; have ready a ladle of cullis, with the heads of a few asparagus, or pease, or any thing else that is in season; make it boiling hot, with the juice of a lemon, and serve it up.

Young rabbits make a good pye in the same way.

PATTEE DES PERDREAUX
A LA CHICOREE.
Partridge pye with endives.

Cut off the pinions of your birds as for roasting, the feet to the knee-joint, tuck the thighs in, and lard them with about six bits of bacon each side, make a little forcemeat of the livers, a little scrap'd bacon, a green onion and parsley, and a mushroom minced fine, and put within-side, lay bottom crust, and your birds in, with pepper, salt, &c., as before, and cover with bacon; fix on your lid, and bake it about two hours; provide some endive cut pretty small, and boil it very tender in a little broth, pour a ladle of cullis, some pepper and salt, and a morsel of shallot; cut up your pye clear of the fat and bacon, boil your sauce a little while, squeeze in the juice of orange and lemon, pour it over your partridges, and serve it up.

PATTEE DES PIGEONEAUX
AUX EPINARS.
Pigeon pye with spinage.

Take about eight small wild pigeons, or as many large squab pigeons, which are best in season, take the livers and make a forcemeat as before, and put it into them, season as the last, cover with bacon, lay them in your paste, and cover them; bake it about an hour and an half, and provide your spinage stew'd nice and green, squeeze the juice well from it, chop it well, put it into a stewpan with a ladle of cullis, a little pepper, salt and nutmeg; let it stew for a few minutes, squeeze in the juice of a lemon; get your pye ready as directed before, and pour it in, and send it up very hot.

DES PETITS PATTES AUX
RIS DE VEAU.
Petty-patties of veal sweetbreads.

For this dish take six small tartpans, if you have nothing for the making such things in, and lay your paste in, provide a couple of sweetbreads, boil them ten minutes or a quarter of an hour, and put 'em into cold water to harden a little, take three or four slices of ham, a mushroom or two, cut all into small dice, and fry in a little scraped bacon with a green onion or two, a little parsley, pepper, salt and nutmeg, get the yolks of three or four hard eggs, and a pickled cucumber or two, and cut to the rest when fry'd a little while very softly; stir all together, and put it into your paste, with a spoonful of gravy, bake them in a brisk oven about half an hour, cut off the lids, and set 'em in your dish, take a ladle of cullis, with a little gravy, a little chop'd parsley, make it boiling hot, with the juice of orange or lemon, pour in into your patties, put on the lids and serve them up.

You may make such a sort of a dish as this almost at any time, with what your house affords, such as the breast of a fowl or chicken, with a slice or two of tongue, a partridge or woodcock, or the like.

N.B. There is a favourite sauce now in high vogue called *a la Benjamelo*; that is as often served with these little matters which shall be given in some of the following receipts.

FILLET DE MOUTON AUX CONCOMBRES OU CELERY.
Fillet of mutton with cucumbers or celery.

Provide one large or two small necks of mutton, cut off a good deal of the scrag, and the chine and splaybones close to the ribs, tear off the fat of the great end, and flat it with your cleaver, that it may lay neat in your dish, soak it in a marinade as before, and roast wrapt up in paper well buttered; for your sauce in the spring or summer, quarter some cucumbers nicely, and fry them in a bit of butter, after laying in the same marinade, stew 'em in a ladle or two of your cullis, a morsel of shallot or green onion, pepper and salt, a little minced parsley, the juice of a lemon, and serve it. The only difference between this and the celery sauce is, instead of frying your celery, boil it very tender in a little water, or broth if you have plenty, and stew it for a quarter of an hour; be cautious you don't break the cucumbers.

CARET DE VEAU A LA CHICOREE.
Neck of veal with endive sauce.

Provide a nice white neck of veal, cut off the scrag, &c., as from the mutton, lay it to soak in such a marinade as for your loin of veal an hour or two, roast it with lards, or slices of bacon, to preserve its whiteness, and send it to table, the sauce under or upon it, which you like best, made just in the same manner as the celery sauce; but for either of these things, in the season, you may use pease, tops of asparagus, kidney beans, bits of artichoke bottoms or cauliflower; and if care is taken they are pretty dishes.

COTE DE BOEUF GLASSEE
AUX EPINARS.
A rib of beef glasse with spinage.

Provide one of the prime ribs, trim it neatly, and lay it in a marinade for an hour or two; take a stewpan exactly its bigness, put a slice or two of bacon at the bottom, lay in your beef, and cover it with the same; to season put in an onion or two, some bits of carrot, a little sweet basil, thyme and parsley, a little pepper, salt, and a blade or two of mace; let it stew gently till it is very tender; take it out upon a plate, strain your braize, clean it well from the fat, put it into a clean stewpan, and boil it with a ladle of gravy very fast, and you'll find it come to a sort of a gluey consistence, then put your beef in, and keep it hot till your dinner-time, and serve it up with spinage done in the same manner as that for the ham.

At another time you may serve it with savoys or red cabbage stript fine and stewed, after being blanch'd, only adding a bit of bacon, with a few cloves stuck in it in the stewing, but not to send to table.

Fillet de boeuf, or fillet of the surloin is done pretty much in the same way, marinaded and roasted, with bacon over it, and the same sort of sauces.

HARICOT DE MOUTON
AUX CARROTS.
Haricots of mutton with carrots.

The old fashioned way of doing this dish, in my opinion, is a very bad one, and not only so but a very expensive one. Two or three fat breasts I have seen provided, cut into pieces ugly enough, and stewed three or four hours, in what I called before, a braize: a sauce is prepared for it, and the mutton again stewed in it, and as much fat sent to table as sauce. For this large dish I would advise the cook to take the best ends of two necks, take two bones to a cutlet, cut one off, and flat it well (I mean the cutlet), tear off the fat from the three or four bones of the prime end, trim them nearly, and fry 'em a few minutes over a brisk stove; for your sauce take the scrags and make a gravy, season in the same way as for that in the second receipt; make a cullis of it with a little flour stirred over the fire with a morsel of butter, pour it to your mutton, and stew it till it is tender; cut your carrots, boil them in water for a while, and put them to it, with some pepper, salt, and a bit of shallot; when dinner-time throw in some minced parsley, squeeze in some lemon-juice, lay your cutlets in the dish, and serve it up.

This is frequently done with small onions fry'd brown, or turnips cut in little square or round bits.

FAISANT A LA MONGELAS AUX FOIS GRAS.
Pheasant a la mongelas with fat livers.

Provide a large pheasant, cut off the pinions as to roast, and with the liver make such a forcemeat as you have seen set down before, put it into your pheasant, and spit it, with some lards of bacon and paper, take care you roast it nicely, and prepare your sauce as follows; take some fat livers of turkeys or fowls, blanch them till thoroughly done, and pound 'em to a paste, put to some gravy and cullis, mix it well together, and pass it through an etamine; cut off the flesh of the pheasant, slice it very thin and put to it, and preserve the carcass hot; add to your sauce, which should be about the thickness of your cullis, a little pepper, salt, some minced parsley, and the juice of two or three oranges; and if you approve on't you may strip a few morsels of the orange-peel in, and serve it up with the hash poured over the breast, and garnish with some oranges in quarters.

UN CHAPON OU DEUX POULARDES, SAUCE RAGOUT MELLEZ.
A capon or two poulets, with a ragout mellez.

Take a large capon or two poulets, and blanch nicely in a morsel of butter or scraped bacon, but cut off your pinions and feet, and tuck in the legs: prepare your ragout in manner following; get a sweetbread of veal, or two of lambs, the fat livers of a turkey or fowls, some cocks stones, three or four mushrooms, a thin slice or two of lemon, blanch all well with a knot or two of eggs, cut all into very small dice, and stew in a ladle of cullis; and you may add to it three or four gizzards and a few cocks combs boiled very tender; fill up the bellies of your fowls or capons, and sew up at both ends, but make a reserve of some of your ragout to pour over; put 'em upon a lark-spit across, and tie upon another, lard them with bacon, cover with paper, and roast them softly, that they may be nice and white, strew in a little minced parsley, a morsel of shallot, squeeze in the juice of a lemon or orange, and serve up with the ragout under. – Remember to draw the threads out.

DES PERDREAUX AU CELERY BLANC.
Partridges, with celery sauce white.

Take three partridges, and make a forcemeat of the livers as before named, and put it into 'em, blanch 'em in a hot marinade, spit them across, and tie them upon another, put on some lards of bacon and paper, and roast them softly; for your sauce, take the hearts or white of six or eight heads of celery split two or three times, and cut to pieces about an inch long, blanch it a minute or two in water, then boil it in some good broth for an hour, put in a bit of butter mixt with flour to thicken it; prepare a liaison, or four or five yolks of eggs and some cream, a little pepper, salt, nutmeg and minced parsley, pour it to your sauce boiling hot, move it for a moment over your stove, squeeze in the juice of a lemon or orange, draw off your partridges, and dish them up with your sauce neatly over them. – This is an excellent sauce for boiled partridges or chickens, done in the same way as above prescribed.

DES BECASSES AUX ORANGES.
Woodcocks, with orange sauce.

Two brace of cocks I think is not too much for a dish as is here proposed; draw them without cutting off the heads, preserve the ropes and livers for a forcemeat to put withinside, twist the feet back and truss 'em neatly with the beak thro' the thighs, and tie the feet upon the vent, spit them upon a lark-spit across upon another spit, and roast them with lards of bacon; when roasted dish 'em up, and cut a gash or two in the breast of each, squeeze upon them the juice of two or three oranges; your sauce must be a clear gravy with a morsel of shallot pepper, and salt; under each cock put a nice toast well soak'd in a hot cullis, and serve them up.

Snipes make a neat dish this way; but I shall make a reserve of them for an *Hors d'oeuvres*.

UN LIEVRE EN CASSEROLE.
A hare stewed.

One seldom sees a hare drest by the English any other way but roasted, or boiled with onions, so that if a gentleman kills sixty or seventy brace in a season he has no variety, and always stands in his bill of fare, a hare; no more. In this we are beat again. One good way, I presume, is this [. . .] Take a young hare (a leveret is another thing) and cut into ten pieces, the two legs, two wings or shoulders, the chine in four, and the stomach and skirts in two, don't blanch them, but skim your wine, &c., well; put it into your stewpan, with about three half-pints of Port wine, two or three onions, a carrot or two, some sweet basil, thyme and parsley, and a ladle of gravy, a little salt and pepper, a clove or two, and a bit of mace, and let it stew gently for two hours, take out your hare clean into another stewpan, and strain your sauce to it, adding a ladle of cullis, and if not thick enough put in a bit of butter and flour, and boil it a minute, and keep it hot till your dinner is ready, fling in a spoonful or two of capers, some minced parsley, and the juice of a lemon or orange, and serve it up with some fry'd bits of bread in the dish and round it. – I hope nothing is said disagreeable or in prejudice of our English and plain way of dressing a hare, for I think it best; but variety adds beauty to a table. I have seen salmon, turbot, soles, &c., frequently served to a gentleman's table in the same one-way till they have come back almost untouch'd, till the end of the seasons, another cook has come along, changed their dresses, and by adding some little matter, and not a jot has remained in the dish; but yet in my opinion not so good. It is in this as it is in dress or equipage, sometimes white pleases best, and sometimes red, and so on to all the colours you can name.

UNE MATELOTTE DES PETITS POULET AUX CHAMPIGNONS.
A matelotte of chickens with mushrooms.

Cut your chickens as for a fricasee, the legs and wings, pinions, breast and back in two, blanch them in water for two or three minutes, put 'em into a stewpan, with a bit or two of ham, a ladle of gravy and cullis mixt, season with a bunch of onions and parsley, a little sweet basil, a morsel of shallot, pepper, salt, a blade of mace; stew all together gently for an hour.

N.B. This sauce may serve for several good uses; but for your matelotte prepare it with a ladle or two of your cullis, with a few nice button mushrooms, put in your chickens, and stew all together, with a little pepper, salt and nutmeg; add the juice of a lemon or orange, and serve it up. The reason of changing the sauce is, that your dish may have a decent appearance: your mushrooms would be broke, and your herbs, &c., by so long stewing be crumbled, and spoil the beauty of the most favourite dish of all.

This is often done with pease or tops of asparagus.

DES ROULADES DES LAPREAUX, SAUCE A L'IVERNOISE.
Rabbits collared, with a sauce a l'ivernoise.

Two couple of young rabbits for this dish I think is not too many: take care to take the bones out quite up to the wings or shoulders, but leave them on with the head; prepare a nice hot forcemeat of some bits of the rabbits that may be spared, a bit of veal or lamb fat, a little scrap'd bacon, a morsel of green onion, a mushroom, pepper, salt, and a little parsley, fry all together for a few minutes; put it into a mortar with some soft of a French roll soaked in cream or milk, a little nutmeg, pound all well together with the yolks of two or three eggs; spread your rabbits in a dish, and lay your forcemeat on, roll them up to the wings, and bind with a bit of packthread; stew them in a braize about an hour and an half, and prepare your sauce thus: 'Tis a sort of a *sauce hachee*, as you have seen before, only to this you cannot put too many sorts of strong herbs, such as tarragon, pimpernel, thyme, marjoram and savoury, a green onion or two, mushrooms, and a bit of shallot, all minc'd very fine and separate; to a ladle or two of gravy and cullis mixt, put in just as much of each as will make palatable in boiling a quarter of an hour with pepper, salt and nutmeg, and a spoonful or two of good oil, throw in a handful of capers, clean your rabbits well from grease, add the juice of a couple of lemons or oranges, and dish up, with your sauce over.

UN PETIT COCHON DE
LAIT EN BALON.
Small fat pig en balon.

SAUCE EN RAVIGOTTE.
Sauce in ravigotte.

'Tis not a common thing to see a pig dressed among us any other way than roasted; but if variety can please I beg leave to send one to table in the following fashion: Cut your pig open from head to tail, but not touch the skin on the back, cut the head close off, and bone the rest, cut off the superfluous bits and make a forcemeat, as in the receipt before, spread it regular, and cut some long thin bits of ham, the yolks of two or three hard eggs, and a bit of green pickle, cover all in with the ends and skirts of the pig, and tie it up quite tight in a thin cloth, just cover it with water well seasoned with onions, carrots, leeks, herbs and parsley, salt, whole pepper, and a little spice; let all simmer together for about two hours; prepare the sauce with a ladle or two of cullis, take a little pimpernel, a few leaves of sage, a mushroom or two, and some parsley, mince all separate, and boil all for a quarter of an hour; put in a small spoonful of mustard, squeeze in the juice of lemons or oranges, take out your balon nice and whole, wipe it with a clean cloth, and dish it up, pouring your sauce over it; don't let your sauce boil after the mustard is in, 'tis apt to make it bitter. – If the balon should open tuck in the skirts under, with a spoon or point of your knife, that it may go decent to table.

Hors d'Ouvres

The next thirty dishes, or thereabouts, are what the French call *Hors d'ouvres*, dishes of a small size, that are generally placed round the outer parts of the table, for first course dishes.

DES PALLETS DE BOEUF AU VIN DE CHAMPAGNE OU VIN DU RHIN.
Pallets of beef, with Champagne or Rhenish wine.

Two or three pallets is enough for a small dish, scrape them clean, and boil for an hour in water, put them into cold a while, and peel the skins off, stew them in a braize till very tender, drain well from the fat, and cut them into pieces as nigh as you can in length two inches, in width one, put them into a stewpan with a small ladle of cullis, a little pepper, salt, and a morsel of shallot, stew all a few minutes with a glass of either of the wines, throw in a little minced parsley, juice of a lemon or orange, and serve it up. This is often sent to table with some onions fry'd nice and brown.

DES TRANCHES DE FILLET DE
BOEUF, AU JUS CLAIR ET ROCOMBOLE.
Slices of fillet of beef, with clear gravy and rocombole.

A pound of meat is enough for this dish; cut it into bits about an inch thick, and flat it down with your knife or a light cleaver; it is better than slicing; make it very thin and jagg it with the back of your knife cross and cross, rub a large stew-pan with butter, a little green onion and parsley minced, fry your beef briskly for two or three minutes, tossing it that it may be done on both sides, take it out into a small stewpan, and pour in a ladle of nice gravy, a little pepper, salt, a morsel of shallot and parsley, boil it but a moment; when dinner is ready squeeze in a lemon or orange, and send it to table.

The inside fillets of loins of mutton or pork is done in the same manner; and though they seem but trifling matters, yet if care is taken to make them very thin, and nicely fry'd, and not boiled too much afterwards, they are good and pretty dishes.

DES QUEUES DE MOUTON A LA
BRAIZE, SAUCE AUX CAPRES.
Sheeps rumps a la braize, with a sauce of capers.

Do your rumps down very tender in a braize, trim them nicely, cut all the ragged bits off, and place 'em in a stew-pan, pour in a ladle of cullis, a spoonful of capers, a morsel of shallot and minced parsley; boil all a few minutes, take the fat clean off, add the juice of a lemon or orange, and serve it up.

Lambs rumps done in this way make a very neat dish, and you may serve either with carrots or turnips neatly cut and fry'd, instead of capers.

DES RIS D'AGNEAUX AUX POINTS D'ASPERGES.
Lambs sweetbreads, with tops of asparagus.

Blanch your sweetbreads, and put into cold water awhile, put them into a stewpan with a ladle of broth, with pepper, salt, a small bunch of green onions and parsley, and a blade of mace, stir in a bit of butter with flour, and stew all about half an hour; make ready a liaison of two or three eggs and cream, with a little minced parsley and nutmeg; put in your points of asparagus that I suppose to be boiled, and pour in your liaison, and take care it don't curdle; add some juice of lemon or orange and send it to table. You may make use of pease, young gooseberries, or kidney-beans for this, and all make a pretty dish.

DES OREILLES D'AGNEAUX A L'OSEILLE.
Lambs ears, with sorrel.

In London such things as these, or calves ears, tails, or the ears of sheep ready for use, or perhaps in some other great markets, are always to be had of the butchers or tripemen.

About a dozen of lambs ears will make a small dish, and they must be stewed tender in a braize; take a large handful of sorrel, chop it a little, and stew it in a spoonful of broth and a morsel of butter, pour in a small ladle of cullis, a little pepper and salt, and nutmeg; stew it a few minutes, and dish up the ears upon it, nicely twisted up.

DES PALLETS DE VEAU AU VIN DE CHAMPAGNE.
Veal pallets, with Champagne.

Provide about two pallets, and boil half an hour, take off the skins, and cut them into such pieces as your pallets of beef, put them into a stewpan with a glass of Champagne, a little minced green onion, parsley, pepper and salt, toss it often till the wine is gone, pour in a ladle of your cullis mixt with gravy, stew 'em softly in it till very tender, dash in a small glass more of your wine, add the juice of a lemon or orange, and send it up.

UNE FRICASEE DES LANGUES DE VEAU AUX ASCHON FLEURS.
A fricasee of calves tongues, with cauliflowers.

Get two tongues, which is enough for a small dish; boil them till the skin comes well off the ragged parts, and slice them very thin, put into a stewpan with a ladle or two of broth, and put in a bunch of onions and parsley, a blade of mace, pepper and salt; let all stew softly till very tender, and liaison as before prescribed, pour it in when boiling hot, cover it close, and let it remain so till your time of dining; move it upon a stove for a minute or two, squeeze in a lemon or orange, and dish it up.

DES OREILLES DE VEAU
AUX LAITUES.
Calves ears, with lettuce.

Six ears will do; stew them very tender in a braize, and your lettuce must be done thus, take as many as you have ears and blanch them in water, open the leaves, and put into each a bit of the middling bacon, with a clove or two stuck in each, close the leaves over, and bind with packthread, put them into a stewpan with a ladle of your cullis, and a little gravy, pepper, salt, and a morsel of shallot, stew them till very tender; take your ears out, and clear them from grease, and put them to your leaves, add the juice of a lemon, and serve them up; take care your lettuce are preserved whole, and laid between the ears.

Lambs ears may be done so, too.

DES RIS DE VEAU AUX
CHAMPIGNONS.
Veal sweetbreads with mushrooms.

Provide two or three veal sweetbreads, blanch them, and cut them in slices, get a few nice button mushrooms cleaned upon a bit of flannel, put them into a stewpan together, and let them stew gently for half an hour in a ladle of cullis, but put no gravy, for the mushrooms will produce some liquor, take a knot or two, or the yolks of three or four hard eggs, dash in a glass of white wine, a morsel of green onion and parsley minced fine, pepper, salt, and nutmeg, squeeze in the juice of a lemon or orange, and serve it up.

Lambs sweetbreads just so.

DES QUEUES DE VEAU AUX CARROTS.
Calves tails with carrots.

SAUCE BRUNE.
Brown sauce.

Cut the tails into two or three pieces, and you must stew these in a braize, and cut the carrots into neat genteel pieces, blanch them a few minutes, take the tails out, and soak the fat well off, put them into a stewpan, with a ladle or two of cullis, carrots, a bunch of basil, onions, thyme and parsley, pepper, salt, a blade of mace, and a clove of rocombole, stew all till your carrots are tender, sprinkle in a little minced parsley, take out the rocombole and herbs, add the juice of lemon or orange, and send it to table.

DES CERVELLES DE VEAU AU RIS.
Calves brains with rice.

The brains of two heads is enough for a good dish, but an Hors d'oeuvres in particular, blanch them, and take off the little bloody fibres, cut into two pieces each, and soak them in a marinade of white wine and vinegar, &c., for an hour, put them into a stewpan with some cullis and gravy, and stew them softly about half an hour; boil your rice in water a few minutes, strain it off, and stew it in broth till it is tender, with a little salt and a bit of mace, dish up the brains, and pour some of the sauce to the rice, squeeze in a lemon or orange, and pour over for serving to table.

When you procure two or three pairs of eyes they make an excellent dish done in the manner of doing the sweetbreads.

DES CERCELLES AUX OLIVES.
Teals with olives.

Two is enough; when you draw them save the livers, and make a little forcemeat, adding some scrap'd bacon, a mushroom or two, a pretty many herbs, pepper, salt, some shallot, all minced, and well mixt, put into the bellies of your fowls and fasten them up; fry them gently a little while in a hot marinade, and spit them across your spit upon a lark-spit, cover with bacon and paper, and roast them, but not too much; prepare your sauce with a ladle of cullis and gravy mixt, pepper, salt, and shallot, and about a couple of dozen of olives pared; draw off your teals, and put them into your sauce, cut them first down the breast, stew about five minutes; squeeze in plenty of orange, with a few strips of the peel, and send to table.

DES PERDREAUX EN RAGOUT,
AUX ORANGES.
Partridges in ragout, with oranges.

Truss your partridges, and roast in the English way, only use no flour; make a sauce of the livers pounded, and add two or three of chickens, put it into a stewpan with a green onion or two, a mushroom, pepper and salt, and parsley;

boil all in cullis a few minutes, and strain through your etamine; cut the partridges as for a fricasee, and put to your sauce; let it boil but just long enough to make the meat hot through, strip in a morsel or two of the peel, a bit of minced shallot and parsley, squeeze in a good deal of juice, and dish it up. Garnish with oranges in quarters.

DES PERDREAUX HACHEE, SAUCE AU ROCOMBOLE.
Partridges hash'd, with rocombole sauce.

Truss these as to roast them in the English way; make a forcemeat with the livers, &c., and roast gently with a lard of bacon and paper, lodge a bit or two of rocombole upon the breasts, and when done, cut all the flesh from the breasts, and cut it in slices thin as possible; keep your carcasses hot, and provide a sauce for the hash, with a ladle of cullis, minced rocombole, pepper, salt, and nutmeg; boil this a few minutes, and put in your hash; when your dinner is ready put it to the sauce; make it only boiling hot, throw in a little parsley, squeeze in some lemon or orange, and dish up upon the bones or carcasses; put enough of your cullis that some may flow over into the dish.

Woodcocks make a good dish done in this fashion.

SALMIS DES BECASSES.
Salmy of woodcocks.

For this too the French truss their cocks in the English way, and half roast them, without flour; cut them in fricasee pieces, and take care to secure all the inside except the gizzards and galls, which you must be sure to take clean away, but the ropes, livers, &c., pound to a paste, with a morsel of shallot, green onion and parsley, pepper, salt, and nutmeg, put in a ladle of your cullis, a glass of red wine, and pass it thro' your etamine, pour it into a stewpan to your meat, let it stew very gently for three quarters of an hour, fling in a little minced parsley, the juice of an orange, and serve it up garnish'd with fry'd bread, and some bits in the dish.

Any sort of birds, such as snipes, quails, &c., that are not drawn, make a pleasing dish done in the same manner.

DES BECASSES FARCEZ, AU JUS CLAIR.
Woodcocks with forcemeat, with clear gravy.

For this you should draw your cocks, cut off the feet, and truss the thighs in; preserve the ropes for the force-meat, and make a little mince of your livers, with a morsel of ham, seasoned with a mushroom, pepper, salt and parsley; cut almost all the meat from the breasts of your cocks, cut it in little bits with the ropes, scrape a little bacon and fry it, seasoned with a mushroom or two, a bit of green onion, a little parsley, pepper, salt, and nut-meg, and put to the soft of half a roll soak'd in cream; mix all well with two or three eggs, fill up the breasts in shape as they were, nigh as you can, brush them over with egg and crumbs of bread, and bake them in a slow oven; and for your sauce have ready some clear gravy,

with a little shallot, pepper and salt, squeeze in the juice
of an orange, and serve them up hot.

POITRINE DES POULARDES
A LA BENJAMELE.
Breast of fowls a la Benjamele.

Two fowls make two dishes, but in different ways; cut off
the legs whole with the feet, and the next shall give directions how to manage them. But the breasts you must
roast, but without the pinions, they may serve for something else; when roasted, take off the skin, and cut off the
white flesh, slice it in thickish pieces, put it into a stewpan, and provide your sauce as follows; take about half a
pint of cream, a bit of butter mixt with flour, put in a
green onion or two whole, a little parsley, pepper and
salt, stir it over a slowish fire till it boils to its thickness,
and pass it through an etamine, put it to your fowl in a
stewpan, and then boil it till it is hot through; add nothing more than the juice of an orange, and send it up.

This sauce may serve for any sort of white meat, and
is now very much in fashion.

DES PETITS BALONS AUX CUISSES
DES POULARDES.
Balons of legs of fowls.

This is to be done with the four legs; take out the thigh
and legbone to the knee, without cutting the skin; let the
feet continue on, and scald or burn off the stocking, but
take care not to burn or scald the skin, for it is to be

sewed up; lay them a little while in a marinade of white wine and vinegar, &c., prepare a forcemeat, such as is for several things before, and spread over the insides; draw them up nice and round, and stew them in a little braize for an hour, or a little more; make a neat sauce of a ladle of cullis and gravy, a dash of white wine, a bit of shallot and parsley minced; take your balons out upon a cloth to drain, and clean from fat; dish them up with the feet to them; boil your sauce a minute, and squeeze in the juice of an orange or lemon, and send it up.

DES PIGEONNEAUX A LA DUXELLE.
Pigeons a la duxelle.

Four or five pigeons will do for an *Hors d'oeuvres*; but this is most times served for an *entree*; cut off the feet and pinions, and slit them down the breast, then take out the livers, and flat them with a cleaver; make a hot marinade of some scraped bacon, seasoned with a mushroom or two, green onions, pepper, salt, thyme and parsley, and a little nutmeg; fry all a few minutes, and let the pigeons be heated through in it, and let them remain till you put them upon your gridiron; take a thin slice of ham for each pigeon, and put them broiling with the ham always at top; I mean when you turn your pigeons, turn your ham upon them; for your sauce, take a ladle of gravy, some sweet basil, a little thyme, parsley, and shallot, minced very fine, a few slices of mushrooms, boiled all together a few minutes; dish up your breast downwards, let your ham continue upon them, and pour your sauce over, with the juice of a lemon or orange.

N.B. There's another way of doing this dish, by tying a slice of veal on one side of the pigeon, and ham on the other, and done in a braize; but it is very troublesome and expensive, and I think not better.

FRICASEE DES PETIT POULETS, AUX CHAMPIGNONS BLANC.
Fricasee of chickens, with white mushrooms.

Cut your chickens as before directed, and blanch them in water, only wash off the skim and soil neat and clean, (for the goodness of this dish half depends upon its decent appearance); any body can make it taste well, but it must be a good cook to make it look well; put a bit of butter in your stewpan, just melt it, and put in your chickens, and shake in as much fine flour as will thicken about a pint of broth, keep it toss'd over your stove two or three minutes, and pour in your broth, but keep it moving for a while that it may not be lumpy, put in a bunch of two or three onions and parsley, a little pepper, salt, and a blade of mace, stew it softly about an hour, provide a liaison of three or four eggs, with a spoonful of broth and cream, nutmeg and parsley; put in a few stew'd button mushrooms; make it boiling, and put in the liaison, give it a toss, cover it close till dinner is ready, squeeze in a lemon or orange, and serve it up.

Instead of mushrooms you may put points of asparagus, young pease, and sometimes without either.

DES BECASSINES AUX FEUILLES DE POURPIER.
Snipes with purslain leaves.

Draw your snipes, and make a forcemeat for the inside, but your ropes preserve for your sauce, spit 'em across upon a lark-spit, covered with bacon and paper, and roast them gently; for your sauce you must take some prime thick leaves of purslain, blanch them well in water, put them into a ladle of cullis and gravy, a bit of shallot, pepper, salt, nutmeg and parsley, and stew all together for half an hour gently, have the ropes ready blanch'd, and put in; dish up your snipes upon thin slices of bread fry'd, squeeze the juice of an orange into your sauce, and serve it up.

DES PETITS RISOLES DE BECASSE, OU BECASSINES.
Risoles of the flesh of a woodcock, or snipes.

Take the flesh from your woodcock, or snipes, and make a forcemeat as follows: Chop your flesh and rope raw and separate, a bit of ham cut very thin, cut into slips, and then into as small morsels as you can, a bit of good sewet, a bit of a manchet soak'd in gravy, season with a bit of green onion, sweet basil and parsley, and a jot of rocambole, pepper, salt and nutmeg, mix all well together, (but not pounded) with an egg or two; lay it in lumps upon a nice thin paste, and make them in the shape of a raspberry or quince puff, but very small; when your dinner is almost ready, provide a large stewpan with lard, and fry all at once; then serve them hot to table without any sauce.

DES PETITS PATTEES EN TIMBAL.
Petty pattees in cups.

SAUCE A LA BENJAMELE.
With a Benjamele sauce.

These are made in copper cups lined with a thin paste; take the breast of a roast chicken, partridge, or a sweetbread blanch'd, and cut into small dice, a slice or two of ham cut in the same manner, two or three girkins, a mushroom or two, or green morelle, fry all this together gently in a little scraped bacon, seasoned with a bit of shallot, green onion, pepper, salt and nutmeg; when cold fill up your cups, and cover with the same paste, bake them gently about half an hour; prepare your sauce, *a la Benjamele*, as for the breast of a fowl. Dish them up bottom uppermost; cut a lid off, and fill them up; take care it is sent very hot to table.

DES FILLETS DES SOLES AUX FINES HERBES BRUNE.
Fillets of soles, with herbs in a brown sauce.

Skin your soles both sides, and lay them a while in a marinade of white wine, &c., dry them well in a cloth and fry them without butter or flour, of a nice colour; take off your fillets nicely, cut them into pieces in length about two inches, put them into a stewpan with a glass of Champagne or Rhenish, pepper, salt and nutmeg, a small ladle of gravy and cullis mixt; mince separate, a green truffle or mushroom, a leaf or two of pimpernel, a little sweet basil, thyme and parsley, and a morsel of shallot; put into your gravy, &c. such a quantity of each as you like best; stew all together very gently for a quarter of an hour, squeeze in the juice of a lemon or orange, and serve it up very hot.

The fillets of plaice tenderly handled make a pretty dish in the same way; the flesh is not so firm as soles, which is my reason for this caution. If *maigre* days, instead of cullis or gravy, make a sauce of such small fish as is before prescribed, or a cullis of crawfish.

FILLETS DES MERLANS MARINEZ ET FRITE AU PERSIL.
Fillets of whitings marinaded, and fry'd with parsley.

The fillets of about six smallish whitings is enough; each makes but two from top to bottom; lay them in a marinade of wine, &c. about an hour, dry them well, and toss them in a heap of fine flour, provide a large stewpan of lard, make it hot, and fry all together upon a brisk fire, fry your parsley crisp and green, and serve your fish up upon it. This is a most favourite dish, and generally eat with the juice of an orange or lemon; but some choose what the French call *sauce pouvrade*, or *sauce poure-homme*, which shall be seen by and by provided for the roast and *entremets*.

FRICASEE DES TENCHES, AUX
FOIS DES MERLANS.
Fricasee of tench, with whitings livers.

In the whiting season you may have plenty of livers at any fishmonger's shop, and a vast addition it is to the goodness and beauty of any dish of this sort; split your tench, or a brace, according to the size; take out the backbone, and cut the flesh in pieces, so as to make them answer, if you have occasion, to your soles or whitings, toss them up in a bit of melted butter oiled, and a little flour, for a minute or two, pour in a ladle of broth, and a glass of white wine, keep it moving upon the stove till ready to boil, and season with a bunch of green onions and parsley, some mace, pepper and salt, blanch your livers, and stew all together about half an hour; have ready a liaison as before mentioned for fricasees, and just before your dinner-time pour it in, and cover it close; before you send it up give it an easy move over the fire for a moment, add the juice of an orange or lemon, and serve it up.

The heads and melts of your fish are favourite bits; so take care they are among the rest.

N.B. The fillets of weavers, perch, soles, or any such firm sort of fish, make a good fricasee, and done in the same manner.

DES PERCHES A L'HOLLANDOISE.
Perch in the Dutch fashion.

Crimp your perch only one gash from end to end, put them into spring-water half an hour, put them into a stewpan with a large glass of white wine, half as much vinegar, plenty of mace, a little pepper and salt, and a bunch of onions and parsley, and some thyme tied together; let them stew gently in this (turning of them once) about twenty minutes, pour as much hot water in as will fill your dish, with a piece of butter mixt with flour, and boil a few minutes longer, take out your herbs, and serve it up with a heap of parsley-leaves over it boiled nice and green. According to my judgment this is a good and delicate dish, and much the best way of dressing perch.

Gudgeons are done in the same manner.

FILLETS DES MAQUEREAUX AU FENOUILLE AND GROSSEILLES.
Fillets of mackerel, with fennel and gooseberries.

For this the French always boil their mackerel as we do, only adding a little vinegar and a bunch of herbs, take the sides of fillets from the bone, and cut in two pieces; about four is enough for such a dish as here proposed, put them into a stewpan with the melts and roes whole, dash in a glass of white wine, a ladle of cullis and gravy, some minced fennel, green onion and parsley, pepper, salt and nutmeg; stew all about eight or ten minutes; put in about half a pint of scalded young gooseberries whole, squeeze in a lemon or orange, and serve it up hot.

Entremets

Next are the *Entremets*, or second course dishes, of which I shall put down about forty of the most fashionable; and give a hint of the management of the roast. By roast I mean what is served for second course, such as a leveret, woodcocks, snipes, or partridges, &c. but no large things, and the sauces they usually serve with 'em. As to pastry things I shall put but few, for I think the English in most of them excel.

DES ALUMELLES D'AGNEAUX MARINEZ AND FRITS, AU PERSIL.
Lambs-stones marinaded and fry'd, with parsley.

In this dish too, if the French are not too cunning for us, they are more modest, and give it a prettier name; blanch them, and take off the outer skins, lay them in a marinade of white wine and vinegar, &c. an hour, dry them in a cloth, tumble them about well in flour, and fry them of a nice colour, and serve them up with no other sauce but parsley nicely fry'd, under and over them; and if well done it makes a pretty dish for second courses.

DES PIGEONNEAUX AU SOLEIL.
Pigeons au soleil.

For this generally is provided squab tame pigeons; blanch them, and stew about an hour in a braize, make them very dry and clean from fat and soil, and make a batter of nothing more than ale or small beer with flour and a morsel of butter oil'd and put into it well stirred together, have a large stewpan of lard ready, dip in your pigeons without cutting off either heads, legs or wings, and fry them of a fine colour, and serve them to table *comme les alumelles*, with parsley. *Sauce pouvrade, sauce pauvre homme*, or *sauce Roberts*, should be always ready in a boat or cup, if any of the company should ask; and I'll put 'em down before I finish.

DES RIS DE VEAU ROTIS,
AUX ASPERGES.
Roasted sweetbreads, with asparagus.

Two good sweetbreads are enough for this small dish; blanch them, and lay them in a marinade as before, spit them tight upon a lark-spit, and tie them to another, a slice of bacon upon each, and covered with paper; when almost done take that off, and pour a drop of butter upon them, with a few crumbs of bread, and roast them of a nice colour; take two bunches of asparagus, and boil, not so much as we boil them to eat with butter; dish up your sweetbreads and your grass between them, take a little cullis and gravy, with a jot of shallot and minced parsley, boil it a few minutes, squeeze in the juice of a lemon or orange, and serve it up.

RAGOUT MELE,
AUX ASPERGES, OU POIS.
Ragout mele, with asparagus or pease.

For this dish you may preserve enough of matters you have to make your dish; you should provide two or three livers, a knot or two of eggs, some morsels of ham, cocks-stones and combs, well stewed; add to this a few mushrooms or morelles, and season with a little shallot, parsley, and pepper and salt; pour to all this in a stewpan a ladle of gravy and cullis; let all stew together for about half an hour; put in the juice of a lemon or orange, and serve it up hot with or without orange as you like best.

DES FOIS GRAS FARCEZ.
Fat livers with forcemeat.

Four or five large livers of turkeys will do for this dish; blanch them in water two or three minutes, and make a forcemeat of some livers of chickens, a bit of ham, a mushroom, a morsel of onion and parsley, pepper, salt and a few crumbs of bread, grate in a little nutmeg, mince all fine, work it up to a paste with a couple of eggs, and fill up the open part of your livers, and make them nice and plump, brush over with an egg, and some crumbs of bread, and bake them half an hour in a gentle oven; for your sauce take a ladle of cullis and gravy, three or four thin slices of ham, a little pepper and salt, a morsel of shallot, boil all about five minutes, squeeze in a lemon or orange, and send them to table with the ham upon or between them.

DES OREILLES DE COCHON A LA ST. MENHOULT, LES PIEDS FRITS.
Hogs ears a la St. Menhoult, the feet fry'd.

One pair of feet and ears for this is quite enough; blanch them in water, split the feet, and with a couple of slices of bacon, and a flat stick like a bit of a lath, tie them together again to keep of a neat shape, stew them in a braize separate from any thing else, till they are very tender, strip the ears as fine as possible; and for your sauce take a large onion cut very thin in slices, and fry brown in a bit of butter, strain them off, and put them into a clean stewpan to the ears, with a ladle of cullis, a dash of white wine, pepper and salt; let it stew a quarter of an hour, with a morsel of shallot, a spoonful of good mustard, squeeze in a lemon or orange, add a little minced parsley, and dish up with your feet fry'd in the same manner as your sheeps rumps, to lay round.

DES OEUFFS A LA PROVINCALE, AU COULIS.
Eggs a la provincale, with cullis.

Take eight or nine eggs (leave out two or three of the whites) and beat them well, put in half a ladle of cullis, a morsel of green onion and parsley minced, pepper, salt and nutmeg, stir it over a slow fire till it is thick enough in the dish, squeeze in the juice of a lemon or orange; dish it up; garnish with some bits of bread fry'd of a nice colour.

DES OEUFFS AU MIROIR.
Eggs au miroir.

For this you must have a dish that will bear the fire, rub the bottom with a bit of butter or oil, sprinkle a morsel of green onion and parsley minced, a little pepper, salt and nutmeg, set your dish upon a chaffing-dish of charcoal, break in as many fresh eggs as will almost fill it, pour over them as much cream as your dish will well hold; when it is just boiling dash with a spoon the cream over the tops, that they may be equally done, squeeze in the juice of an orange or lemon, and serve it up.

DES OEUFFS AU SOLEIL.
Eggs au soleil.

Poach about eight fresh eggs very nicely, take them out into cold water (not draw cold water to the hot, for in a moment they'll all stick to the bottom), lay them a while in a marinade of a glass of wine and vinegar, &c., dry them upon a cloth, prepare a batter of ale, &c. as before prescribed, fry them nicely in lard, and serve them up upon a deal of fry'd parsley.

DES OEUFFS SAUCE
A LA BENJAMELE.
Eggs sauce a la Benjamele.

Poach about as many for this dish and order in the same manner; but be sure they are fresh; for, from the experience I have had, I am sure it is not in the power of the best cook in the kingdom to poach stale ones handsome, notwithstanding they may come all whole out of the shell; get your sauce as before mentioned, put the eggs in when it is only warm, and just before you serve it to table squeeze in the juice of an orange or lemon, give it a moment's heat; dish up, pouring over the sauce, and a small pinch of pepper upon each egg.

DES OEUFFS POCHEZ
AU JAMBON MINCEZ.
Eggs poached, with a sauce of minced ham.

Poach some eggs as before; for your sauce take two or three slices of boiled ham, or a slice or two raw, and well blanched, mince it very fine, a mushroom, a girkin, a morsel of onion, a little parsley, pepper and nutmeg; stew all together a quarter of an hour; when it is your time of serving to table, let your sauce be about half boiling, and put in your eggs, squeeze in the juice of an orange or lemon, dish up, and pour your sauce over.

This is a good dish with tops of asparagus, or pease done in manner like this, leaving out the minced things. There are numberless ways of dressing eggs, so that it would be endless to put all down here. Eggs with gravy, spinach, sorrel, asparagus, broccoli, are pretty second course dishes, and many others that I could name; but they are grown so very common I shall not give them place here.

DES EPERLANS AUX ANCHOIS AND CAPRES.
Smelts with anchovies and capers.

About eight large smelts is enough for a little dish; for your sauce boil a couple of anchovies in a glass of Rhenish or other white wine till it is dissolved, and strain to a ladle of cullis and gravy, season with a bunch of onions and parsley, a blade of mace, and a bay leaf or two, pepper and salt, put your fish in, and let 'em stew gently about a quarter of an hour, take out your onions and parsley, and throw in a spoonful of capers, make all boiling hot, squeeze in some juice of orange or lemon; take your fish out to dish up, very tenderly, fling in a little minced parsley to your sauce, and pour it over; garnish with orange or lemon in quarters.

You cannot name a small freshwater fish that is not good done this way.

DES GOUJONS EN GRATIN, AUX FOIS DE MERLANS.
Gudgeons en gratin, with livers of whitings.

About a quarter of a hundred of gudgeons will do; provide for your sauce a few livers of whitings; if not to be had easily take the liver of a skaite or thornback, thoroughly blanch it well, take a ladle of cullis and gravy, an onion or two, some parsley, a bit of mace, pepper and salt, and a mushroom, put in your liver or livers, boil all a quarter of an hour or so, and pass it through an etamine, put it to your fish, and stew them gently fifteen or twenty minutes, squeeze in the juice of a lemon or orange, dish up your gudgeons in neat order, and pour your sauce over.

This is best where plate is used, and done over a chaffing-dish, that the sauce may stick to the bottom, and moistened afterwards with a little gravy; it takes its name from that, and an excellent sauce it is for such little matters; and, was I a gentleman, I would keep two or three silver dishes in my house, if it was for no other use but this; and some little creams require it too, which you will have among these entremets.

DES ECREVISSES AUX OEUFFS DE MER.
Crawfish, with the spawn or eggs of a lobster

A quarter of a hundred of crawfish is enough for this dish; take the shells off from the tails and the small claws, pound them well with some of the spawn (the inside spawn is best to add to the colour) pour to it a spoonful or two of broth or gravy, with some cullis, and rub it well through an etamine, put it to your fish, with a blade of mace, pepper and salt, a little nutmeg; stew all together a few minutes, squeeze in the juice of a lemon or orange, and serve it up.

DES CREVETTES AU BEURRE.
Prawns with butter, or buttered prawns.

Take the tails only of the prawns, and peel them, pick out the little sand bag or maw from the body, and pound them all with a little pepper and a morsel of onion and nutmeg; put into them a spoonful or two of broth, and pass through an etamine; to two ounces of good butter add as much fine flour as will thicken it, toss it over a stove two or three minutes, squeeze in the juice of a lemon or orange, and send it up hot.

Small lobsters make a very pretty and good dish done in the same manner, but be sure you take out the maw of the body and gravelly gut of the tail, or you must spoil your dish.

On fish days make a little broth of fish.

DES ECREVISSES DE MER FARCEZ DANS LES COQUILLES.
Forcemeat of lobsters in the shells.

Two middle-sized lobsters will do for this dish; take the tails with the soft part of the insides, and chop very small, put to it the flesh of a plaice, and pound all together, but only to mix it well, grate in a little nutmeg, pepper, a spoonful of oil and vinegar, minced parsley, the soft of a bit of bread soak'd in broth or cream, a couple of eggs, stir all well together, cut the body shells in two pieces long-ways, trim them neatly, and fill them with your forcemeat, brush them over with a little butter and egg, strew a few crumbs of bread over, and bake them in a slow oven about half an hour; squeeze on the juice of orange or lemon, and serve them up hot. Taste this before you put it into the shell, for it may not be salt enough. The reason of omitting this ingredient with shellfish is, they are always boiled in salt and water.

DES PETITS POIS A LA CREME.
Pease with cream.

Let your pease be very young, put them into a stewpan with a bit of bacon with some cloves stuck in, pour in a ladle of broth, a bunch of onions and parsley, pepper, and a little salt if it is required, stew them gently till almost dry, take out the bacon and herbs, and put about a gill of cream, a bit of butter and flour mixt, let it go gently on about ten minutes, squeeze in the juice of lemon or orange, and dish them up very hot. Sometimes I have seen Mr. Clouet put in a bit of fine sugar, and in the English way of stewing pease I have never seen it done without.

Des pois aux laittues brune; pease with brown lettuce differs only by chopping some cabbage-lettuce and mixing with them, and instead of cream use a ladle of cullis. But the Old English way of dressing pease with a bit of good butter I think is still the best.

DES ASPERGES AU JUS CLAIR.
Asparagus with clear gravy.

For this, trim and scrape your grass neat and clean, set them over the fire in but little cold water and salt: the reason of this is, the French prefer a crispness and yellow in asparagus and French beans, to what we are always in so much care to make green and tender; but they eat it (as they do many other vegetables) for a hot sallet; boil your grass but a little time, and serve them to table with nothing but gravy and the juice of oranges or lemons.

French beans whole are done in the same manner frequently.

DES HARICOTS AU BLANC.
French beans, with a white sauce.

For this the French cut their beans as thin as possible, and boil as we do in a vast deal of water, with salt, to preserve their greenness, but not so tender, strain them off, and put 'em to a small ladle of broth, put in a small bunch of green onions and parsley, with a little pepper and salt, just bring it to boiling; prepare a liaison of eggs, &c. and pour in, toss it over the fire a minute, add the juice of a lemon or orange, and serve it up.

DES CHAMPIGNONS EN FRICASEE.
Fricasee of mushrooms.

Clean some nice button mushrooms with flannel and water, wash them in a second, and put them into a stewpan, with a glass of Champagne, Rhenish, or other white wine, a bunch of onions, thyme and parsley, pepper, salt, and a blade of mace, toss them up in this upon a stove a few minutes, and pour a small ladle of broth, with a bit of butter mixt with flour; let all stew a quarter of an hour, take out your herbs, have ready a liaison as before, and just before your dinner-time pour it in, move it gently over the stove a minute, squeeze in an orange or lemon, and dish it up.

Green morelles are done in the same manner, and give an excellent flavour in all made dishes and force-meats, but they are not to be had but a month or two in the year. Your dry'd morelles and truffles from abroad are like what we call a chip in potrage; they do neither harm nor good.

DES TRUFFLES AU VIN DE FRANCE.
Truffles in French wine.

Truffles in England are a very scarce commodity, and of consequence very dear; but are sometimes to be had. I have known some found in the neighbourhood where I live, but very bad, and not much preferable to a potatoe. The good and best are from some part of Italy, where they make dishes of them many different ways; but the only method of dressing of them here is, first of all to lay them to soak some time in water, and brush them with a hard brush, for they grow in a stiff clayey ground, so that it is no easy matter to make them clean. Put them into as much claret or Burgundy as will cover them, a large onion or two, a bunch of herbs, whole pepper, salt, and some spices; let 'em simmer gently for about half an hour, and send them to table hot in a napkin; pepper and salt is the general sauce for them; preserve your wine they are boil'd in, it gives an excellent flavour to cullis or gravy, &c.

DES CARDONS, SAUCE PIQUANTE.
Cardoons, with piquant sauce.

Cardoons are a thistley sort of vegetables, and an exotick plant, and are managed in the garden as celery or endives, by being mouldred up as they grow in height to make them white. The French make use of this in some sort of sauces in the first-course dishes instead of celery, &c. But for an *entremets*, or second-course dish, they generally do it in the following manner: One large one is enough for a small dish; cut the white part only in pieces about two inches long, blanch it in water, and if you have a braize tie it up, and stew it very tender in that; if not take broth, season it high, and stew it in that; take it out upon a cloth, and pull off the skin on both sides, and put it into a sauce piquant, as before mentioned; let stew softly twenty minutes or half an hour, squeeze in the juice of a lemon or orange, and dish it up. This is very good sauce for roast beef or mutton.

DES SHERDONS, A LA BENJAMELE.
Sherdoons, a la Benjamele.

This is a plant of our own, and grows common upon dry banks and barren ground, but worth nothing for this use till improved by the gardener, which is done by transplanting, and earthing up to whiten, and when peeled, and brought to market, looks more like fine endive than a common thistle. The English always plain boil it, and have butter only for sauce; but foreigners with the sauce above, or a brown sauce of cullis or gravy; boil it in a little broth, pepper and salt, but not tender; pour that from it, and put your white sauce, let stew a few minutes, squeeze in an orange or lemon, and dish it up. Whole heads of celery and endives are often done in the same way for these *entremets*; and most foreigners eat heartily of them.

DES ARTICHAUX MARINEZ
AND FRITS.
Fry'd artichokes marinaded.

Trim them to the sound part of the bottom, and cut off the small leaves round, cut the points of the others to about an inch above the bottom, cut them in small pieces, and take out the choke or seedy part, lay them to soak in a marinade of white wine and vinegar, &c. often moving them; prepare a batter of beer and butter, dry them well, and fry all at once, and send them up upon a heap of fry'd parsley. Fry sometimes with flour sticking to the marinade, and sometimes without any.

DES QUEUES D'ARTICHAUX,
SAUCE BRUNE.
Bottoms of artichokes, with a brown sauce.

Cut off all the black and soil from the bottom, trim round the sides, but not through the heart of the leaves, cut off the tops of the leaves almost to the bottom, so as to leave a hollow; when your choke is taken out, boil them in water till you find the inside, put them into cold water, and with your finger scrape it out to make 'em white and tender; prepare a hot marinade of boiling water, a lump of butter and flour mixt, a bit of sewet, a lemon peeled and sliced in a little salt, an onion and a bunch of herbs; a little soup-pot is best for this; when it is well mixt and boils, put in your bottoms, and let them simmer sideways till very tender, and they will grow white as a curd; for your sauce take a ladle of cullis, and add to it such sorts of herbs as you like, pepper, salt and nutmeg; boil all a little while, take out the bottoms upon a cloth to drain, dish them up, squeeze the juice of an orange or lemon into your sauce, and send to table.

Here seems to be a vast deal said upon such a trifling matter; but I have been in hundreds of kitchens where there never was a cook that could cut an artichoke-bottom genteelly, or make it white; and there cannot be a prettier dish; and you may serve them to table with a white sauce of any sort, or with plain butter only.

DES LAITTUES FARCEZ.
Lettuce with forcemeat.

Blanch your lettuce, and open all the leaves to the heart; take a forcemeat such as is before provided for such little things; put as much into each as you can close; put them into a stewpan with as much broth as will cover them, put pepper, salt, some pounded mace, a bit of butter and flour; provide a liaison of egg and cream, &c., use them easy, squeeze in the juice of a lemon or orange, and dish up hot. Another time make a brown sauce.

DES EPINARS A LA CREME, AUX OEUFFS, OU DU PAIN FRIT.
Spinage with cream and eggs, or fry'd bread.

This being a pretty genteel dish, it is pity to leave it out. Scald it in a morsel of butter and water and salt, press the juice from it very dry, chop it small, and put it into a stew-pan with about half a pint of cream, a morsel of butter and flour, a whole old onion, pepper and salt, a little nutmeg; stew all together a few minutes, take out your onion, squeeze in a lemon or orange, and dish it up. Garnish with either hard eggs cut in two, or bits of bread nicely fry'd.

UNE CREME A L'HOLLANDOISE.
A Dutch cream.

Provide as much cream as will fill your dish, boil it with sugar, a bit of lemon-peel, and some coriander-seed, let it stand to cool, with a quart of cream, take the yolks of ten eggs, make them smooth and put to your cream, rub it through an etamine, have a stewpan of water boiling, put your dish upon it to touch the water, pour in the cream, cover with another dish, and watch when it is settled, set in some cool place, and send it to table, you may colour it with a hot iron if you like. This and the next are often served upon the middle of the table, which is supposed to be a large dish, then take the whites of the eggs, whisk them up to a nice froth, and gently lay on your cream, sift a little fine sugar upon it, colour and take the rawness of the eggs off with a salamander.

UNE CREME VELOUTEE AUX GESIERS.
Cream made with gizzards.

Provide as much cream for this dish as is necessary. Without the help of eggs, boil it with such ingredients as the other, but add a pinch of salt, get the gizzards of three or four chickens, take only the skins within side, wash and dry them, that you may roll them to powder, put them into your etamine, and pour in the cream, pass it through three or four times; prepare your dish upon boiling water as before; the moment you see it coming to a curd take it off, and set it in a cool place. This is a pretty *entremets*, and when you would make use of it for a large dish whisp up a little cream into a froth, and serve it up.

Creams of tea, coffee, chocolate, &c., are done in the same manner, only take care you boil them well in a little of your cream, that they have the full flavour.

DES BIGNETS DE POMMES
A LA BAVARRE.
Apple fritters a la Bavarre.

Pare and quarter some large pippins, lay them to soak in brandy, fine sugar, cinnamon and lemon-peel, and toss them often. Your dinner being almost ready, dry them in a cloth, tumble about well in fine flour, and fry them all very tender in hogs lard; dish them up, and sift plenty of fine sugar over them, colour nicely with a salamander, and send them up.

DES BIGNETS DE PECHES,
AU VIN DE RHIN.
Peach fritters, with Rhenish wine.

This must be done with peaches of the fleshy sort, and cut in two, put them to some Rhenish wine as long as you please, with plenty of fine sugar, cinnamon, and lemon-peel, dry 'em, and fry without any flour, strain your wine into another stewpan, and boil it to a caromel; dish up, and pour it over with the kernels of the peaches blanched, split, and thrown in.

Apricots, or any sort of large good fruit, are done in the way as before, with this difference only; you must be very cautious to use them tenderly, and fry them in a thin batter of small beer and flour: there is a fleshy nectarin that makes a fritter, but they too must be fry'd in this batter, for the skin won't bear the violent heat of the lard.

DES BIGNETS DE GELEE
DE GROSSEILLES.
Fritters of currant jelly.

Of these there are several sorts; but the favourites of Mr. Clouet were one of the pastry sort, and the other I'll shew in my next. Provide a nice rich paste, and roll out very thin; brush it all over with egg, and lay your jelly down in little lumps as many as you may want for a little dish; prepare another sheet of paste, and lay it over, pressing well between, that it may not come out in frying; make your lard pretty hot, and fry of a fine yellowish colour, and dish them up with some fine sugar sifted over.

DES BIGNETS DE GROSEILLES
EN SURPRIZE.
Currant fritters en surprize.

The difference between this and the last is this: instead of paste, cut some bits of wafer-paper, and lay some little lumps of jelly upon each, wet round the edges with a little water; but close them up as you go; have ready a thin batter of small beer or ale, and some oiled butter; have your fat ready heated, and put them to fry immediately; take this care and you will make a pretty dish, and serve them up with sugar sifted over.

DES BIGNETS DE CERISES AU FOUR.
Cherries in a French paste.

For this you must have a conserve of cherries, and your paste make as follows; take half a pint of water, put to it a morsel of fine sugar, a grain of salt and a bit of lemon-peel, an ounce of butter, and boil it a minute or two, take it from your fire, and work in as much fine flour as it takes to a tender paste, put one egg at a time and mould it well till it comes to such a consistence as to pour with the help of a spoon out of the stewpan upon a tin or cover, covered with flour; scrape it off in lumps upon tin with the handle of a large key, and bake them of a nice colour and crispness, cut a hole in the bottom, and fill up with your conserve, sift some sugar over, and dish up.

If you make this paste according to the rule before you, it will swell very large and hollow, and makes a genteel *entremets*.

DES POIRES A LA PORTUGUEUSE, AUX GROSEILLES SECHES.
Pears Portuguese fashion, with currants.

Take three or four *boncretiens*, or other good winter pears, pare them, cut them in two, and take out the choke, boil them in water only half an hour, put them into a stewpan, pour in a pint of Port wine, with a lump of fine sugar, a stick of cinnamon, a bit of lemon-peel, a spoonful or two of water, and about five or six ounces of the best dry currants; let all stew together till your pears are very tender; dish them up, and pour your currants over, but take out the cinnamon and peel.

The French make several sorts of amlets of eggs; but in these matters I think we beat them all to pieces, except one, and that is this.

UNE OMELETTE A LA NOAILLES.
Amlet a la Noailles.

For a small dish take the yolks of about eight fresh eggs, but save the whites; make the yolks nice and smooth, with a quarter of a pint of thick cream, strew in some sifted fine sugar, crumble in a few drop-cakes or fine biscuit, and a little nutmeg; a few minutes before your dinnertime, whisk up your whites, and stir all together well, moisten your frying-pan first with lard, and made very hot, and pour it in, have a bit of butter by you, and stoop round upon your trevet to do the sides first, move the edges with the point of your knife, and put in some morsels of butter; when it is pretty well set, lay the edges as far as you can to the middle, make it round, and turn it bottom uppermost in your dish, sift on some sugar, and serve it up hot; garnish with orange. Your chief care must be to prevent its sticking to the bottom, fry it nicely, and you will find it a very handsome and good *entremets*.

This may be made with a savoury sauce by putting cullis of meat or fish, with their proper seasonings, instead of cream, &c.

DES MACARONS A LA CREME.
Macaroons with cream.

These are to be had at any confectioner's shop in London, and the newer they are the better; boil them in water only till very tender, to half a pint of cream put half a small spoonful of flour, some sugar and nutmeg, with a morsel of salt, stir it over the fire till it is thickish, cool it, and put in the yolks of three eggs, and a morsel of oiled new butter, stir it well together, and put in your macaroons, put a nice little rim of paste round your dish, pour in your ingredients, and put it to bake about a quarter of an hour, and take care it is of a fine colour; sift a little sugar over it, and serve to table.

This is not what we call macaroons of the sweet biscuit sort, but a foreign paste, the same as vermicelly, but made very large in comparison to that.

DES ANCHOIS AU PARMESAN.
Anchovies, with Parmesan cheese.

Fry some bits of bread about the length of an anchovy in good oil or butter, lay the half of an anchovy, with the bone upon each bit, and strew over them some Parmesan cheese grated fine, and colour them nicely in an oven, or with a salamander, squeeze the juice of an orange or lemon, and pile them up in your dish and send them to table.

This seems to be but a trifling thing, but I never saw it come whole from table.

DES OLIVES A LA ROCOMBOLE.
Olives with rocombole.

Take the fleshy part from the kernels, as many as will do for your dish, blanch them a minute or two, put them into a stewpan with a ladle of cullis and gravy, mince in some rocombole and parsley, pepper, salt and nutmeg; let them stew but three or four minutes; dash in a glass of white wine, a spoonful of good oil, squeeze in plenty of lemon or orange, and serve them up.

This too is an *entremets* that is much eat among foreigners, and the English seldom miss of coming in for a share of it.

Thomas Gray's Recipes

[These recipes were written by the poet Thomas Gray on the blank pages of his copy of William Verrall's *Complete System of Cookery*.]

TO DRESS A CARP (ISAAC WALTON'S RECEIPT)

Take a carp (alive if possible) scour him clean with salt and water, but scale him not; then open him and gut him. Save the blood and liver, and put them with the Fish, into a small kettle. Put in sweet marjoram, thyme, parsley, of each ½ a handful, a sprig of rosemary and another of savoury, bound up in 2 or 3 small bundles, 4 or 5 whole onions, 20 pickled oysters, and 3 anchovies. Pour in as much red-wine as will just cover him. Seasoned with salt, cloves and mace, orange and lemon-peel, cover the pot and set it over a quick fire. When boiled enough, melt a quarter of a pound of butter with half a dozen spoonfuls of the broth, the yolks of 2 or 3 eggs, and some of the herbs shred. Lay him in the dish with the broth, and pour the sauce over him. Garnish with lemon.

TO DRESS AN EEL (SAME)

Wash him in salt and water, pull off the skin as far as the vent, take out the guts clean, but wash him not within. Scotch him in 3 or 4 places with a knife, and put into the belly and into the scotches sweet herbs cut small and mixed up with an anchovy, butter, salt, and a little nutmeg. Then cut off his head and pull the skin again over him, tieing it tight at the end to keep in all the moisture. Tie him to a spit with tape, and roast him leisurely, basting with salt and water till the skin breaks and then with butter, no other sauce than what was within, or has drop'd from him.

TO DRESS MINNOWS, LEACHES, ETC. (SAME)

Wash them well in salt, cut off the heads and tails, and gut them, but do not wash them afterwards, then fry them with yolks of eggs, cowslip or primrose-flowers, and a little tansie.

VEAL STEW'D WITH RICE (MRS. SUTTON)

Boil the veal, till it is enough, with an onion in it, then take it out; and strain off the broth, put the rice into it and a little mace, and let it stew till it is done enough; thicken it up with a little flower and butter; put the veal into the rice to warm, and serve it up; half a pound of rice is sufficient for 4 pounds of veal.

TO DRESS LARGE ROACH OR DACE
(THE BEST WAY).

Lay them without scaling on a gridiron over a slow fire, strewing on them a little flower. When they begin to grow brown make a slit along the back only skin-deep, and lay them on again. When they are enough, the skin will peel off clean and entire from the flesh: then open the belly, and take out the inside. Sauce anchovy and butter.

TO DRESS A CHUB.
(IS: WALTON'S WAY).

Scale, wash, and gut him clean, making the hole as small, and as near the gills as you can, but above all clean the throat perfectly from all weeds and grass, put sweet herbs into the belly, and tie him with 2 or 3 splinters to a spit, roast him, and baste often with vinegar (or verjuice) and butter, and good store of salt. It must be dressed the day it is caught.

TO DRESS A PIKE

Open him at the gills, take out the guts, and keep the liver, which is to be shred small with marjoram, thyme, and a little savoury; put to this some pickled oisters and two or more anchovies (both these last whole) add a lb of butter, and salt sufficient, and mix with the herbs, with a blade or two of mace: sow all up in the belly close, thrust your spit through the mouth and out at the tail. Do not scale him. Take 4 or 5 thin lathes, and tie them with tape round his body long-ways to prevent his breaking off the spit. Roast him very leisurely, often basting with claret, butter and anchovy, in taking off the tape preserve him entire. Then to the sauce in the pan and within him, add butter sufficient with the juice of 3 or 4 oranges. You may rub the dish with garlick.

CUCUMBER SAUCE

Pare and slice them, then beat and squeeze them dry in a coarse cloth. Flower and fry them brown, add a little gravy, some claret, pepper, salt, mace and nutmeg, some butter worked in flower, and toss them up thick. They are sauce for mutton or lamb.

OXFORD PUDDING

Take grated bread, shred suet, pick'd currants, sugar, of each a quarter of a pound, mix together: grate in a good deal of lemon-peel and nutmeg. Break in two eggs, stir all together, tie in a fine cloth, and boil ½ an hour or more.

HUNTING PUDDING

Half a lb of flower, as much Suet shred, ½ a lb of Currans wash'd and pick'd half a quarter of a lb of raisins, three eggs, some lemon-peel and nutmeg grated, a gill of cream, two spoonfuls of sugar and one of brandy. Boil it.

STUFFING FOR VEAL OR
CALVES-HEART

Take a pickled Herring, skin, bone, and wash it in several-waters, chop small with ½ a quarter of a pound of suet, some bread grated fine, parsley cut small, a little thyme, nutmeg and pepper to your taste, mix it with two eggs (tried, and found bad).

CAVICHE (FROM L*D* D*RRE*)

Take three Cloves, 7 scruples of Coriander-seeds bruised ginger powder'd and Saffron, of each half a Scruple, three Cloves of Garlick, infuse them in a pint of good white-wine vinegar, and place the bottle in a gentle heat, or in water to warm gradually. It is to be used, as Catchup, in small quantity as a sauce for cold-meats.

TO DRESS TROUT
(C. COTTON'S RECEIPT)

Take a trout within 5 hours at most after it is caught, wash and dry it in a napkin, then open and take out the guts and all the blood, wipe the inside very clean without washing, notch him (on one side only) in three places to the bone. Put into a kettle as much hard stale beer (but not dead) vinegar, a little wine and water, as will cover the fish, a good deal of salt, a lemon-peal, a handful of sliced horse-radish, a little bunch of rosemary, thyme, and savoury. Let the fire be quick, and when the liquid boils to the height, put in the fish. While it is doing, beat up some butter with a ladleful of the liquor it boils in, and when done enough, pour over it for sauce, strewing on a little powder'd Ginger, and plenty of horse-radish shaved. Garnish with sliced lemon. Dress a Grayling in the same way, but scale it first: a Trout is never scaled.

SAUCE FOR A SHOULDER
OF MUTTON

When it is three parts roasted, put under it a plate with a little water, 2 or 3 spoonfuls of Claret, some sliced onion or shalot, a little grated Nutmeg, one anchovy washed and minced, a little bit of butter. Let the meat drop into it, and when it is enough, run the sauce thro' a sieve, and put under it, with a little elder-vinegar, or

Take the same ingredients, with the juice of an orange: stew them together a little; and pour to the gravy, that runs from the meat.

A GENERAL SAUCE

Take a little lemon-peal minced fine, nutmeg, beaten Mace, and shalot. Stew them in a little white-wine and gravy, and melt your butter therein, if for fish, add anchovies, and oyster liquor.

TO BOIL PLAISE OR SOLES

Put salt, whole spice, white-wine, and a bunch of sweet herbs into water, and (when it boils) a little vinegar. Let it boil apace, and then put in the fish, boil them till they swim, then take up and drain them well. Take a little of the liquor, butter and anchovies, beat up thick over the fire, and pour it on the fish with lemon and minced parsley.

BUTTERED LOBSTER, PRAWNS, OR SHRIMPS

Take out and mince the meat. Stew gently with some white-wine, salt, and a blade of mace. When very hot, put in some butter and crums of bread. Warm the shells and fill them with it.

FRIED LOBSTER

Slice the meat long-ways; flour it, and fry crisp in butter, beat up some butter, with the inside bruised, a little shallot, nutmeg, and claret; when ready, squeeze in an orange, and pour it over.

SAUCE FOR BOILED MUTTON

Take a piece of liver, the size of a pidgoen's egg boil it tender with half a handful of parsley to a little thyme take the yolks of 4 hard-eggs and dissolve them with one anchovy, some beaten pepper, and nutmeg, and salt, a glass of white-wine, and the gravy that drains from your meat. Beat it up thick with butter, and when hot, add a small spoonful of vinegar.

TO MAKE GRAVY IN HAST

Slice an Ox-kidney, season well with salt and pepper, just cover with water, put in a bunch of butter, and let stew gently.

SAUCE FOR STEAKS

A glass of ale, 2 anchovies, a little thyme, savoury, parsley, nutmeg. and lemon-peel shred altogether. When the steaks are ready pour out the liquor, and put the ale &c. into the pan with some butter rolled in the flour and when hot, strain it over the steaks. Have a care the ale is not bitter.

ORGEAT (FROM MR. MASON, LD D.*RE*)

Take Jordan Almonds 1 lb, Bitter Almonds 1 oz or something less, or (instead of them) Apricot-Kernels about 1 oz. Blanch them all, and throw away all that are rotten or worm-eaten, beat them very fine in a stone-mortar: when you begin to beat them, put a cupful of water to them to prevent their turning to oyl. As they grow dry in beating, continue to add a little water to make them beat more easily. When they are fine, put them in an earthen pan, and pour on by degrees 2 quarts of spring-water, stirring them about with a spoon, that they may mix well and not in lumps. Take two lemons, and rub them gently on some fine sugar (not too hard least you make them bitter) sweeten to your palate, and put a tablespoon-full of orange-water to it. Drain it through a fine hair-sieve, and when it has drain'd once, pour it gently over the almonds again, for it will be too thick with only once draining.

CURRY (GOV^R FLOYER'S RECEIPT)

Take 2 lb of Beef, 2 lb of Veal, to 5 parts of water, and let it boil to a quart: an onion stuck with cloves, almonds ¼ of a pound bleached and pounded fine, a table-spoon-full of Turmarick, 8 or 10 Coriander seeds, ½ a spoon-full of Cumin-seeds, a Bay-leaf, Cayon pepper to the taste, a thick slice of Lemmon with the peel on: all these put into the sauce-pan after it is skimmed, and boil together to the thickness of a cream, then strain through a sieve and skim off the fat. Take 2 chickens cut as for a Fricasee, fry them of a light brown and when dried put them into the liquor, and stew till they are enough. Squeeze in half a lemon, skim off the fat again and garnish with lemon and barberries.

Put one lb of rice prickled and washed into boiling water with a little salt: boil till tender, but not too much. Pass it through a cullander, and shake it loose into a dish. Send it up with the Curry, but in a different dish with pickle.

A curry may be made with Rabbits, Veal, Fish, or any thing.

ORANGE POSSET

Mix the juice of three Taville oranges and as many lemons with sugar to a syrup. Put a pint of cream warm (or milk thickened with an egg) into a large tea-pot, and pour from a distance upon it. Let it stand a whole night. Prisk it with sweet-meats and blanched almonds, and serve. (Palgrave).

GREAT  FOOD

THROUGHOUT the history of civilization, food has been
livelihood, status symbol, entertainment – and passion.
The twenty fine food writers here, reflecting on different
cuisines from across the centuries and around the globe, have
influenced each other and continue to influence us today,
opening the door to the wonders of every kitchen.